HOW TO BUILD A
21st CENTURY
FINANCIAL
PRACTICE

HOW TO BUILD A 21st CENTURY FINANCIAL PRACTICE

Attracting, Servicing, *and* Retaining Affluent Clients

MATT OECHSLI

Total Achievement Publishing – Greensboro, North Carolina

Total Achievement Publishing
P.O. Box 29385
Greensboro, NC 27429

Second Edition

Designed and typeset by WMB Design – Greensboro, NC
Cover design by Foster & Foster, Inc. – Fairfield, IA
Printed in the United States of America

ISBN: 0-9656765-0-1

Testimonials
for *How to Build a 21st Century Financial Practice™*

Without question How to Build a 21st Century Financial Practice™ is the most useful guide we have found for our team. You have seen the future and have developed a model that will help anyone in our business develop a team that will meet the wants and needs of the truly high net worth client.

Bruce Arnett
Director
Deutsche Banc Alex. Brown

Matt Oechsli has done a wonderful job in identifying, through original research, the critical services affluent investors demand from financial professionals. He then devised a complete and comprehensive system for the financial advisor in developing long-term relationships with this tremendously important market segment. His book is the ultimate road map to a 21st Century Financial Practice™.

Steven Binder
Regional President, Central Region / Senior Managing Director
First Union Securities

Your advice helped our team focus on providing excellent service to an exclusive client base. This resulted in fewer (but better) client relationships as well as a 100% increase in our fee-based business. Thanks for your guidance.

David J. Bromelkamp, CIMC
Senior Vice President / Investment Officer, Senior Consulting Group
RBC Dain Rauscher

In two years Matt took our team to the next level. His insight and attention to details in a progressive manner helped us build on 25 years of experience, to cut out waste and focus on our main goals. He energized and revitalized us in every aspect of our organization, from advertising to client development. This book will walk you through every step.

Scott Dittrich
Senior Vice President
Tucker Anthony

Matt's ability to capture the true essence of where our industry will be in the future is remarkable. He has hit it right on the head with his book, How to Build a 21st Century Financial Practice™. The successful financial advisor of the future will embrace this book and style of business, thus propelling him as a leader in our industry well into the future.

Mark Casey

The lexicon of the financial services industry has changed forever - from brokers executing transactions to financial advisors providing a wealth management process. So why have few practitioners actually made the transition? I think the principal roadblock has been that brokers haven't been able to visualize how to get from where they are to where they need to be. It has been too theoretical - too fuzzy. Not any more. With his seminal work, Matt provides a step-by-step road map that clearly outlines the path to a more productive financial advisory process, without giving up your day job along the way. Nothing worth doing comes without a price, but waiting for you is a ready market and minimal competition. Plus, the price of ignoring these lessons will be far greater.

Hap Cooper
Director of Private Client Services
Kirkpatrick Pettis

Anyone currently working in the arena of Wealth Management, or considering forming a Wealth Management team, must read Matt Oechsli's How to Build a 21st Century Financial Practice™. This book is actually a "process guide" that can serve both as a road map to follow and a model upon which to benchmark your progress in attracting, advising and retaining Affluent clients.

Charles Grose
Executive Vice President / National Director, Private Client Group
RBC Dain Rauscher

Excellent read! Once again you have jumped into the real keys to success for Advisors! You successfully articulated the problem and the action steps to help advisors achieve in the 21st century. Nice work!

Lou Holland
Managing Director for Nuveen Advisor Partners
Nuveen Investments

Success as a Financial Advisor in today's diverse and complex markets requires both a broad intellectual commitment and a strong understanding of how to attract and keep affluent clients. Many Advisors have found that functioning, as a part of a wealth management team is the optimal way to achieve their desired success. For advisors who have made, or are even considering, the decision to be part of a wealth management team there is no more valuable resource than Matt Oechsli's How to Build a 21st Century Financial Practice™. Matt will show you how to build and operate a team in an efficient and effective fashion that will deliver optimum financial results."

Barry Knight
Senior Vice President / Director of Sales Development
Pioneer Investment Management

A well thought out blueprint for success.

Alex Mihajlov
Branch Manager / Vice President
A.G. Edwards & Sons Inc.

Do you want your financial practice to thrive in the 21st Century? And, do you want balance in your life with time for family and other important activities? If so, then you must embrace Matt Oechsli's How to Build a 21st Century Financial Practice™. It is a user's manual; how-to from start to finish. You will learn all that it takes to transform your practice for the long term. Make no mistake; this is really hard work. But Matt gives you the tools and guidance you need. Let him help you reach your personal dreams while taking extraordinary care of your most special client relationships. No question, a must read for financial professionals!

Robert G. Krebs, Jr.
Vice President, Resident Manager
Merrill Lynch

Matt Oechsli's template for achieving success with wealthy clients in the 21st century is right on target. This book is a must read, and requires a dedicated commitment to implementation for those Financial Advisors who want to prosper going forward. Not taking this book seriously is akin to choosing a horse and buggy over an automobile.

Ben Powell
Vice President and Branch Manager
Morgan Stanley

Acknowledgements

Although there is only one name on the cover of this book, it required the time and talents of a number of people to make it a reality. In effect, it was a total Team effort. I would first like to thank Mike McGervey, Director of Training and Development at The Oechsli Institute. His analytical skills, his ability to assist in writing and rewriting, and his ease in collaborating with the other team members (me), have provided this book with much of its substance.

As editors and proofreaders, Sharon Eagen and Sandy Oechsli have spent countless hours straining their eyes over these words in order to make them more understandable. They would then find themselves debating each change with Mike, who would carry the debate to me, thus ultimately paving the way for what I consider to be a much more readable book.

The clean layout is the handiwork of Marc Barrus. Marc has not only enhanced the utility of the book, he put up with our ongoing changes (thanks to Sharon and Sandy) without a complaint and on deadline. We also are confident you will agree with us that Greg Foster created a superb 21st Century cover design.

Finally, I would like to thank all the financial professionals who have encouraged me to get off my duff and write this book, and have also contributed by way of sharing their fears, hopes, challenges and experiences throughout this project. As financial professionals, you above all deserve to reap the rewards as you work toward developing your own 21st Century Financial Practice.

Table of Contents

Introduction

For here we are not afraid
to follow the truth
wherever it may lead.
Thomas Jefferson

The opportunity to advise the affluent in the management of their wealth has become the pot of gold at the end of the rainbow for many financial professionals. Although it remains an elusive dream for some, there are those who are turning that dream into reality. During the third quarter of 2001, a tough time for the economy, we consulted with Wealth Management Teams who successfully convinced Affluent Investors to transfer assets of 7.5mm, 10mm, 23mm and even 40mm to be served by their management teams.

Where were these affluent clients drawn from? In each case mentioned above, the clients came from a highbrow wealth management firm that was still resting on a reputation gained back in the Gilded Age. Quite frankly, it wasn't all that difficult for them, because each Team had something important going for them – a highly productive Wealth Management Team.

Wealth Management has become the latest catch phrase for the financial services industry. Dissatisfaction among Affluent Investors is unprecedented. The affluent are searching for *unbiased multidimensional solutions* to protect, grow, and distribute their wealth. I emphasize the fact that they do not want a salesperson attempting to provide such advice, but there's more to it than that. They also do not respond well to financial professionals who have been operating in a "one-dimensional" capacity: accountants deal with year-end taxes; insurance agents handle protection issues; stock-brokers manage brokerage investments; Financial Planners create plans; bankers deal with lending; attorneys prepare legal documents. Many are even beginning to question the value received from their highbrow wealth management firm that only offers a limited range of financial management solutions. Which is probably why a VIP Forum study showed that around 50% of all high net worth households use three or more financial professionals. In this scenario, a true Wealth Management Team will have very little competition.

If the opportunity is so great, why does the pursuit of wealth management remain merely a pipe dream for many financial professionals? Is there a proven business model that can be followed?

You Must Follow a Proven Business Model

The operative word is *proven*. We all remember the failure of many dot-com business models that were supposed to be the new path to riches. Much of their failure can be attributed to the fact that those models ignored the tried and true principles of building a profitable business.

In the financial services industry, the challenge has been in trying to adopt the proven wealth management model used by trust companies and elite brokerages to the individual financial professional. MyCFO, a two-year old wealth advisory start-up in Mountain View, California with approximately 300 clients representing over $40 billion in assets at the end of 2000, demonstrated that providing unbiased advice and delivering solutions for the multidimensional needs of their affluent clientele can be highly successful. In their case, it's done on a grand scale with unlimited resources. But now it's your turn to figure out how to do the same thing on a scaled down basis and with minimal investment. Here's how we discovered what it takes to meet that challenge.

Back in early 1999, before there was much talk about wealth management or building Wealth Management Teams to target Affluent Investors, we began to sense that the times, they were a-changin'! Financial Advisors everywhere were telling us that traditional direct mail, cold call and seminar marketing tactics were not working as well as they once had. A growing number were admitting that the Internet was pulling at least some investors away from them. Many complained about having too many clients for them to service adequately, and yet admitted that they were still trying to collect more clients because that's what they had been taught to do. Think about it.

- Too many clients to service adequately.

- Losing clients to an always available, information rich, low cost service – even though it provides no significant human interaction.

- Increasingly finding that old sales and marketing tactics aren't working any more.

At the same time there was tremendous growth of wealth in the United States. In 1996, three years after the introduction of the World Wide Web, *Forbes* reported "Great fortunes are being created almost monthly in the U.S. today by young Americans who hadn't a dime when we created our *400 Richest in America* list 14 years ago." By 1999, the price of admission to the 400 Richest list had grown another 25%. We also kept reading headlines like: "A new millionaire is created every 4 minutes in the United States," or "One in 7 now makes over $100,000 a year," and "The newly rich plus 76 million baby boomers are primed to invest for their retirement." The large trust and investment banks as well as the growing group of full-service Financial Planners were all scrambling to meet their needs, which created an erosion of clients among the brokerage houses. The

Affluent Investor market was growing much faster than the efforts to adequately serve their wealth management needs. What an opportunity!

Then came the BIG question:

Are the men and women who sell and deliver financial products and services throughout the financial services industry prepared to capitalize on that opportunity?

We suspected that they were not. But that was a perception, not a fact, and we wanted the facts. As the 20th century came to a close, The Oechsli Institute commissioned Jacokes & Associates to conduct an independent study of Affluent Investors drawn from a sampling of 10,000 across the United States. The average yearly income of our respondents was $135,000. Our goal was to *uncover what it will take to gain and maintain client loyalty from Affluent Investors in the 21st century.*

There might be some disagreement about our sampling. Does an annual income of $135,000 assure affluence? Not necessarily, and not according to the definitions used by Forbes, as listed below.

Category	Income	Wealth
Superrich *(Affluent)*	$10 million plus	$100 million plus
Rich *(SemiAffluent)*	$1 to $10 million	$10 to $100 million
Upper-Middle Class *(Targeted by our study)*	$75,000 to $1 million	$500,000 to $10 million

Source: Forbes, October 11, 1999

On the other hand, our definition has two advantages. It has a strong probability of being what the Roper Organization refers to as an *Influential American.* Also, this group seems to be the primary target market for financial institutions possessing a retail sales/distribution force. For purposes of simplicity, we decided to refer to this sampling as our *targeted Affluent Investor.*

Results from our research project were startling. With a 95.2% validation factor, survey respondents reported that their financial professional was *not* meeting their expectations in 14 of the 20 qualities they rated as being most important. This alarming gap between performance and expectations certainly signaled serious erosion in client loyalty. We believed that with the changes taking place, it would become an issue of survival for many financial professionals.

Looking for a relevant relationship between what is *important* from the client's perspective and the *actual performance* of their financial professional, we narrowed down the list and focused on specific qualities that showed the most statistically significant gaps between expectations and performance. These are the critical gaps that must be closed if the financial professional hopes to attract and retain Affluent Investor clients by meeting their investment expectations. In fact, our research indicated that at least one-third of the advisor/client relationships we probed were in jeopardy.

Summarizing this in a macro context it becomes very simple, actually basic; Affluent Investors *do not* want a salesperson advising them regarding their finances, period! Unfortunately, they perceive most financial professionals, be they stockbrokers, insurance agents, Financial Planners, personal bankers, etc., as "salespeople."

But this should come as no surprise to a veteran of the financial services industry. The old trappings remain.

- Sales contests are still the norm.

- Offices still conduct weekly sales meetings. Imagine calling your attorney's office only to be informed he/she is in a sales meeting!

- Support personnel are still referred to as Sales Assistants; while attorneys use paralegals, dentists employ dental hygienists, and doctors work with medical assistants and nurses.

- Too frequently the breadth of knowledge is not sufficient to provide advice on the more complex financial affairs of the affluent. And if all of this is not enough, most financial professionals have more clients than they can keep up with.

And so, true to the sales culture from which they were born and bred, they indiscriminately search for more clients, under the guise of targeting the Affluent Investor of course.

But our research also brought GOOD NEWS! Among the Affluent Investors surveyed, 88% did employ the services of a financial professional and 90% claimed they did not use the Internet for serious investment decisions. In other words, they were (and continue to be) ripe for your pickin'! This highly profitable segment of the market wants professional advice and counsel from someone they can trust. In fact, they are searching so desperately for what they perceive as "unbiased" advice and solutions for the multidimensional aspects of their finances, that many experts claim the acquisition cost for these highly coveted clients is zero. Word-of-mouth influence is their primary tool for making these subjective decisions.

From our "right now" research, we were able to identify 12 statistically significant qualities that we later used to shape our *21st Century Financial Practice™* model that is directed toward helping Financial Advisors transition from a sales practice into operating a successful business that targets the Affluent Investor.

As you go back to the beginning of this Introduction and look again at the changes that were gaining momentum during the last two years of the 20th century, you can make no mistake about it; *meeting* and *exceeding affluent client performance expectations is the essential ingredient for the survival and success of any full-service financial professional.*

The three largest performance expectations gaps from our study clearly indicate how critical it is to close these gaps. Here is what Affluent Investors are saying to financial professionals:

- I am not receiving satisfactory *value* for the fees and/or commissions I pay.

- I do not trust the *quality* of the financial advice I receive.

- I do not trust that the financial advice I receive is *always* in my best interest.

Value, quality, and *always* are key Affluent Investor client development concepts for the 21st century because they summarize the essence of those *performance gaps.* The message lurking behind these gaps is that Affluent Investors perceive their Financial Advisors to be salespeople. But to fully understand which expectations Financial Advisors are not meeting, we need to look at the entire list of nine factors. This will serve as the foundation upon which you will build your high net worth Financial Advisory Practice, your Wealth Management Team. From the largest gap to the smallest, Affluent Investors want someone who can:

- Provide satisfactory value for fees and commissions paid.

- Be trusted to give advice that is always in the client's best interest.

- Provide high-quality and trustworthy information for making financial and investment decisions.

- Understand family circumstances when recommending investment actions.

- Always keep promises.

- Continually look for better ways to serve the client.

- Provide timely and accurate response to questions, errors and complaints.

- Explain financial information in language clients can understand.

- Explain clearly how the investor will pay for the services he/she will receive.

Developing strategies and tactical how-to's for overcoming these nine performance gaps is the backbone of our *21st Century Financial Practice™* model.

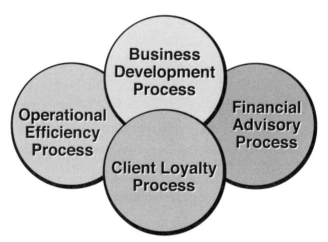

Our research, coupled with more than 20 years of training and coaching financial professionals, led us to develop the *21st Century Financial Practice™* model, which we have used to help financial professionals build Wealth Management Teams that successfully attract, service and retain the loyalty of Affluent Investors. This is the model that successfully guided the Teams mentioned earlier. We visualize this model as four interlocking circles, each representing a key process that has proved to be all-important to achieving that level of success. Everything related to this model is *process* rather than transaction driven. The focus is on doing the *right things*, for the *right people*, at the *right time*, and for the *right reasons*.

Following is a brief description of each *process*.

1. *Business Development Process* (Chapters 3 through 6) – Here you will begin to think more like a businessperson. You will learn how to develop a simple working 5-Year Business Plan that allows the necessary tactical flexibility while maintaining complete focus on your long-term strategy. Linked to this plan will be the profile of the clientele ideally suited to your practice, your *Ideal Client Profile*.

   To make certain that you measure the correct indicators of success, you will also be introduced to a fairly sophisticated business practice for monitoring both progress and results, called a *Metrics Scorecard System*. You will quickly discover that it goes far beyond the simplistic sales measurement of commissions. Next, still within the realm of your *Business Development Process*, you will develop a customized marketing strategy that will enable your Team to attract, qualify, and close Affluent Investors.

2. *Financial Advisory Process* (Chapters 7 and 8) – It's within this process that you will begin to act like a business professional serving a specific market niche – the Affluent Investor. Your first step will be to analyze your performance in the 8 Key Financial Advisory Categories where Affluent Investors need and want solutions. This goes beyond what you might like to do, and deep into what *must* be provided.

   Herein lies the reason, and the best business reason, for determining the Team makeup required to achieve the needed competency to deliver valued service in each of these categories. We will walk you through a simple, but proven procedure for designing your *Financial Advi-*

sory Process, one that will afford you the requisite structure plus the flexibility to personalize every aspect of your services to each client's needs.

3. *Operational Efficiency Process* (Chapters 9 through 12) – This is the arena where you make certain that your actions (*Financial Advisory Process*) are complemented operationally, and that every member of your Team does his or her part to perform them consistently and professionally. In the spirit of becoming an efficient business, we will assist you in realigning the daily tasks of each member of your Practice/Team into Areas of Responsibility.

Linked to this will be the establishment of specific performance standards to ensure that all tasks are performed with FedEx efficiency so that all service is delivered with Ritz-Carlton quality. This requires delegating Areas of Responsibility to Team Members best able to perform that responsibility, and initiating professional development plans to strategically expand each Team Member's knowledge and skills.

4. *Client Loyalty Process* (Chapters 13 and 14) – You cannot develop a healthy position in the mind of your affluent market if you are losing affluent clients. Negative word-of-mouth influence travels at 16 times the speed of its positive counterpart. Frankly, our research and daily contacts indicate that too many of these precious clients are being lost. This must stop, and it will. Because you will learn how to profile each Affluent Investor client's loyalty so that you can determine the specific actions to take in order to enhance value and retain that loyalty. The creative part comes in developing Team strategies for building stronger client loyalty.

It all begins with that 5-Year Business Plan. Our ongoing research indicates that even though 93% of all financial professionals are targeting the affluent, only 20% have a written business plan that goes beyond annual sales targets. Without that written plan, there is no context to give meaning and direction to everything that follows. Notice too that the word Team appears in each description of the *four processes*. The reasons are simple:

- It takes a Team to build a successful *21st Century Financial Practice™* catering to wealthy investors' needs and wants.

- It takes a Team to deliver solutions regarding the multidimensional aspects of your affluent clientele's personal finances. One-dimensional relationships, be they insurance, banking, investments, taxes, etc., are flawed when it comes to working with the affluent. Not only are they too cumbersome, requiring too many people dispensing so-called financial advice, but they also reek of sales.

You don't need to wait for some crystal ball to reveal the future. As a financial professional, your future is *right now*. Our purpose here is to share our findings, both through empirical data derived from research and through anecdotal evidence garnered over the past 23 years of coaching and counseling Financial Advisors. It comes to you in the form of user-friendly instructions that can serve as both a road map and template upon which you can build your *21st Century Financial Practice™*.

Because *Team Building* is an integral part of this process, we will provide you with everything you need to either build a Team from scratch or realign an existing Team into a true Wealth Management Team.

When you have completed the first 14 chapters, you will have an opportunity to bring this future into your real world of today. Chapter 15 will help you use the criteria of our *21st Century Financial Practice™* model to look closely at what you believe is important for your future – and to match what you are currently doing with what you have identified as important. We call that *Benchmarking Your Future*.

In Chapter 16, you will learn to use a powerful technique that, if followed faithfully, will significantly increase the probability that you will never be "caught short" again by the uncertainties of a constantly changing and fuzzy future.

Books provide the greatest benefit when they are read, marked up, set aside while thought over, and picked up again when the reader is ready to continue the thought provoking journey crafted by the author. That is certainly what we want to see happen as you read this book. But even more important, we hope the ideas and insights you discover here will contribute significantly to your future success as a financial professional.

Discovering
Your Future

Chapter 1
Building a 21st Century Financial Practice™

Chapter 2
Why It Takes a Wealth Management Team

Building a 21st Century Financial Practice™

Aim for the highest.

Andrew Carnegie

Welcome to the 21st century! How do you respond to that greeting? Is it "Thank you, I'm excited to be here," or is it more like "Thanks, I guess. I'm feeling a bit uneasy about being here."

At the end of the 20th century, the bull market was charging ahead and folks were saying, "It doesn't get much better than this!" But in 2001 the "better" was gone, and we wondered how much "worse" it could become. Experts scrutinized the reasons and Loren Fox, writing in the March 20, 2001 issue of *Business 2.0* magazine, described the situation this way: "Internet stocks have plunged, venture capitalists have turned thrifty, and the market is allergic to risk." That brief statement neatly characterized the prevailing mood driving business decision making. But more than anything, the suddenness with which the business climate went into reverse is what sobered us all.

That suddenness surprised almost everyone. One-dimensional financial professionals immediately caught the brunt of it from angry clients whose investments "went south," whose tax bite became too great, whose protection was inadequate and whose planning proved to be incomplete. This was especially the case with those clients who took a short-term (shortsighted!) view toward investing. Truth be told, at least part of the blame

---

for this short-term perspective stems from the transaction-based, sales and marketing model that has been the one-dimensional hallmark of Wall Street. But guess what? That too, is changing.

An Industry In Transition

The financial services industry is experiencing a major transformation. The one-dimensional sales and marketing model driven by traditional transaction-based compensation programs is on the way out and is being replaced by a multidimensional fee-based Financial Advisory approach targeted primarily to attracting the Affluent Investor. There are three major factors driving this transformation.

1. First is the tremendous growth of wealth in America. Back in 1982, Forbes identified only 13 Americans as billionaires. As I stated in the Introduction, by 1996 Forbes reported that, "Great fortunes are being created almost monthly in the U.S. today by young entrepreneurs who hadn't a dime when we created our *400 Richest in America* list 14 years ago."

   In 1997, Forbes reported 170 billionaires. In 1998, even though the stock market was down 1% from the previous year, the price of admission to the top 400 had risen more than 5%. In 1999, Forbes noted that "the rich are everywhere," and that "the price of admission has grown another 25%." Again in 2000, there were more rich people than ever before. In early 2001, as already noted, we experienced a serious market correction – and a growing dissatisfaction with everything related to investing. However, with dissatisfaction comes opportunity – and especially with Affluent Investors.

2. A second factor is the impact of Internet technology. Added value services that advisors have depended upon for their bread-and-butter

are fast becoming commodities. Through the Internet, investors have instant, 24/7 access to more and better information and services than any individual broker can readily provide. Low cost investment transactions continue to be a big attraction for many, and Financial Advisory services are becoming only a mouse click away. For example:

- Merrill Lynch, Lehman Brothers, Credit Suisse First Boston, and Morgan Stanley were among the first investment banks to Webcast their own content to larger institutional clients. Merrill Lynch has also introduced this service to retail investors, though the information is not quite as extensive. You can bet that others will follow suit. (Pickering 2001).

- Direct Access provides on-line investors with a screen full of bids and offers coupled with charts, enabling them to select and place orders without having to wait for their on-line broker to do the order placement for them. (Daly 2001).

3. A third factor is the increasing dissatisfaction with professional salespeople attempting to give financial advice while earning a living selling financial products and services. Stockbrokers are now facing what insurance agents have wrestled with for decades, the public perception that they are merely salespeople. Yet, they are also aware of the need for unbiased advice regarding both investment and insurance solutions.

- Our 1999 (Bull Market) Affluent Investor research informed us that the dissatisfaction was strong enough that one-third of the Affluent Investors in our survey were considering dissolving their relationship with their financial professional.

- Our 2000 (Bear Market) Financial Professional research informed us that 49% of those surveyed had lost multiple affluent clients over the previous 12 months. In fact word on the street, anonymous but probably not far off the mark, is that one major wire house lost as many $1 million accounts as it's distribution force opened throughout the calendar year 2000.

As a result, there is a *convergence* occurring. A number of large brokerages are in the process of shifting their business to multidimensional fee-based financial advice platforms to assist their distribution forces in attracting upper-middle class and affluent clients. Large investment banks and private banking companies that have historically targeted only the very wealthy are now vigorously pursuing that same group.

A host of other organizations such as accounting firms, insurance companies, banks, and money management companies are also forming their own Financial Advisory service groups. Their goal is to focus upward toward the more affluent while investment banks reach downward. Even H&R Block has announced their entry into financial planning. The fact is:

Everyone is pursuing the same affluent client with the same "let us be your Financial Advisor" message.

Now, here's the good news. Mark Hurley, chief author of "The Future of the Financial Advisory Business and the Delivery of Advice to the Semi-Affluent Investor" white paper, predicts that the industry will grow tenfold. That represents an incredible opportunity!

It's also interesting to note that in the *Jobs Rated Almanac 2001*, published by the *Wall Street Journal*, Financial Planner was rated number one – while Stockbroker was listed in 90th place. They explained it this way: "If you're looking for the nation's best job in terms of low stress, high compensation, lots of autonomy and tremendous demand for your skills –

look no further than Financial Planner." They went on to say, "Myriad new retirees, aging Baby Boomers, and young dot-com executives are demanding their (Financial Planner's) expert guidance – today, and in the future." In the same rating, Insurance Agent was ranked 133, Attorney 63, and Accountant 18. Along with Stockbroker, these three disciplines play huge roles in the financial planning process.

Building Your 21st Century Financial Practice™

As you ponder your own future, think about it in terms of:

Building a 21st Century Financial Practice™
Committed to developing or restructuring your financial practice to successfully *attract, service, and retain affluent clients* in the highly competitive and ever-changing business environment of the 21st century.

Why should you think in those terms? Here are four important reasons:

1. Unless you are an independent, the company you work for will ultimately make that decision for you. At first, it may seem that there is more talk than action. But that will change – and along with it will come new compensation formulas, new products, additional platforms, and an ever-growing emphasis on Teams.

2. The market potential is difficult to ignore. At the time of this writing, there are about 300,000 American households with a net worth of more than $5 million – another 6 million households with a net worth between $1 and $5 million – and still another 10 million households with a net worth of $500,000 to $1 million. That's a potential market of 16.3 million households.

3. The supply of upper-middle class and affluent people seeking competent unbiased financial advice far exceeds the ability of the industry to deliver that service. Writing in the *Journal of Financial Planning*, Jonathan T. Guyton observed:

"Conversations with established planners around the country routinely reveal that they 'have more clients than they can handle,' 'wish they weren't so busy,' or 'recently raised their minimums to better manage the flow of new clients'."

---

4. Targeting Affluent Investors has significant advantages, especially in times of market uncertainty. In a survey by Phoenix Investment Partners, one-third of the Financial Advisors who responded stated that clients are more difficult to retain today than five years ago. This is especially true of clients with less than $100,000 in investable assets. They tend to focus on the short-run and, due mainly to media influence, are more apt to compare investment results with friends and family. Clients with $1 million to $5 million investable assets are much easier to retain. They tend to be more focused on the long-term, are more experienced, require more services, receive more solutions, and are consequently more disciplined. (Observer 2001)

If these four reasons aren't enough to convince you of the direction you need to go, here is a prediction for you to consider. From our research and experience with Financial Advisors, particularly Financial Advisory Teams, here's how we see it.

Within the next 10 years, we believe the financial services industry will evolve into a relatively simple two-tier structure.

Tier 1: Those who target Affluent Investors. There will be those who work *as* Financial Planners/Advisors and those who work *for* Financial Planners/Advisors. As we will discuss in Chapter 2, the Financial

Advisory Teams who serve Affluent Investors will not only be made up of company employees; they will also include wholesalers, contractors, and alliance partners – and possibly other types of relationships we haven't even thought of today.

Tier 2: Those who will be established in high traffic areas (shopping malls, large retail stores, etc.) to provide financial products and services to middle class and even upper-middle class investors. They will join the insurance, tax, real estate, dental, optometrist, and other professional services that are being drawn to that type of location.

The opportunities for Tier 2 will come from the vacuum created by those in Tier 1 who have set minimum investment levels that middle class and upper-middle class people can't meet. As that vacuum expands, it will also encourage continued development of on-line financial products and services – but with the added dimension of a live quasi-financial professional who facilitates the initial access and use of those products at a location convenient to the client.

What It Will Take

Building a successful *21st Century Financial Practice™* is a challenge. It will take you from 18 months to 2 years of total commitment to take your business to the level of working exclusively with affluent clientele. During that time, you will learn how to significantly increase your revenues while reducing your number of clients. You will also discover that skills and qualities that have made you successful will serve you here as well.

- You will still set goals – but they will be expanded and formalized into a 5-Year Business Plan.

- The discipline you applied to selling and opening new accounts will now become multi-disciplined as you expand the solutions you offer and develop a *Financial Advisory Process* to better service your affluent clients.

- Your willingness to take psychological and emotional risk will now be applied to new areas, often taking you outside your comfort zone.

- Instead of building on your initial investment in your financial sales practice, you will reinvest in expanding your knowledge and skill, in creating new strategies, developing new Team Members, and in employing new marketing tools as you create a true business practice.

In an effort to refocus his team's dedication and effort, a football coach told his players that *success* happens when *preparation* meets *opportunity*. Since you are still reading this, I will assume that you have decided to develop or restructure your financial practice in order to successfully attract, service, and retain affluent clients in the highly competitive and ever-changing business environment of the 21st century. As the insightful football coach so accurately stated, *your success* too will come as *you prepare* to effectively *meet your opportunities*, and this book is written to help you do exactly that.

Again, welcome to the 21st century as you work toward developing your *Wealth Advisory Team.*

Why It Takes a
Wealth Management Team

If we do what is necessary,
all the odds are in our favor.

Henry Kissinger

U.S. Trust was founded in 1853 to work with the affluent in preserving and enhancing their wealth. Although much has changed for U.S. Trust, including a merger with Charles Schwab in June 2000, their focus remains unchanged. They intend to be the premier investment and wealth management firm in the nation.

In their *Annual Review 2000*, U.S. Trust acknowledged the dramatic increase in new competitors targeting Affluent Investors. They also state with an obvious degree of confidence that "…in reality, few firms are able to offer comprehensive wealth management." The review goes on to outline what U.S. Trust perceives as the "True wealth management demands:

- Professional expertise in a wide variety of disciplines, including investment management and consulting, fiduciary services, financial tax and estate planning, and private banking.

- Coordinating and integrating these capabilities to create customized solutions that meet each client's unique needs.

- A dedication to quality service and building long-term relationships with clients that endure from generation to generation."

You can be sure that U.S. Trust services their "family wealth clients" with more than $50 million in assets differently than their "early stages of accumulating wealth" clients who have $250,000 or more to invest. How do you think they are able to provide "professional expertise in a wide variety of disciplines" or "coordinate and integrate these capabilities to create customized solutions that meet each client's unique needs?" You guessed it; it takes a Team. No individual can do all that alone. It takes a Team to build a successful *21st Century Financial Practice™* because everything revolves around the concept of *wealth management* and the multidimensional requirements contained therein.

You can no longer function in the traditional one-dimensional capacity of simply "managing" clients' investments. Affluent Investors want to protect, expand and distribute their wealth effectively; and need a solutions provider for the multidimensional aspects of their personal finances. Within that context, you must work with each client to help them achieve their own unique set of financial priorities and goals. That may include any or all of the following.

- Meet current financial obligations to creditors.

- Reduce debt that cannot be paid off in the current month.

- Eliminate debt within ___ months.

- Maintain or upgrade their lifestyle.

- Provide for their financial security, never being reliant on others.

- Have an ongoing understanding of their net worth.

- Budget what they have coming in and how they use it.

- Minimize the amount of taxes they pay, and pay those taxes on time.

- Insure against serious financial loss due to medical bills and/or not being able to work.

- Insure against serious financial loss from having to replace or repair damage to their home, other real estate, vehicles, and other large tangible property investments.

- Pay for the present education of adult family members and the future education of children.

- Retire by age ___.

- Retire with at least ___% of their current level of income for at least ___ years.

- Have a detailed plan of how and to whom their property, valuables, and money will be distributed upon their death(s).

- Have a charitable giving plan that is consistent with their values and compatible with the rest of their financial needs, goals, and priorities.

Notice that this list is in language your clients understand, not in the technical terms you commonly use. This is the language you must learn to use.

It's also a long list and is not all-inclusive. Imagine sitting down with each client to walk through this list so they can tell you which items are priorities and what specific goals they have for each. Imagine taking those priorities and goals, developing a written financial plan, helping them select and secure the right financial products, and then interacting with each client at appropriate points to help them manage those priorities and achieve their goals. Could you do that alone, or with a Sales Assistant to help you? You know you couldn't.

That's wealth management, and that is what you need to be doing consistently for every client within 18 months to 2 years from the moment you initiate your Team. During this period of time you will need to aggressively transition from the "one-dimensional" role servicing a large and varied clientele, to a "multidimensional" role servicing a limited select clientele. In other words, you will need to build a highly effective Wealth Management Team so that you can compete with other financial professionals who are also competing for the same affluent clients.

Four Levels of Team Formation

Building an "effective Team" is where the challenge lies, and there are far too many who do not understand this. Consequently, we see four *levels* of "Team formation" efforts taking place.

Level 1: "I'll just get me an Assistant or two to relieve my work load."

Even though this level is slowing being eradicated, we still see the evidence of this approach in many places. Following are several *real situations* that are the product of this mindset:

- Mr. Hundred Thousand Dollar account calls. The Financial Advisor is out of the office, so the Sales Assistant takes the call. Mr. Hundred says that he heard from his other broker at XYZ that his NC HFA bonds were called. He continues, saying that he wonders why he hasn't heard from his Financial Advisor (the one he is calling). The Sales Assistant checks and sees the money, and tries to explain why she thinks the Financial Advisor hasn't called. Mr. Hundred says, "Forget it. Just mail me the check – today!"

- A client calls her Financial Advisor who is out of the office. The Sales Assistant answers. The client says that the Financial Advisor promised to wire $50,000 to her two days ago for a house closing scheduled for today. The Sales Assistant looks at the account and sees that it was not done. The Sales Assistant asks the client if she sent an LOA to the Financial Advisor for this transaction. She replies, "No. He didn't ask for one, and I don't care about that. I need that money *now!*"

- A client wants to open an IRA on April 15. His Financial Advisor says that she will be out of the office and to ask for her Sales Assistant or Junior Partner. The client walks in at 3 P.M. on April 15. The Sales Assistant has no clue why. The client hands the blank forms (signature only) to the Sales Assistant. When the Assistant asks the client for the information, the client says he doesn't know. His Financial Advisor had told him to just sign it, and her Sales Assistant would do the rest.

It's obvious that there is no sense of teamwork in these situations. Where this mindset still prevails, Sales Assistants complain that they only do menial tasks such as filing, answering the phone, and getting coffee for their boss. Urgent calls come from clients. The Financial Advisor is out. The Sales Assistant doesn't know when he or she will return and is totally unprepared to answer the client's questions. Or, the Financial Advisor gets a call. The Assistant answers the phone and tells the Advisor who it is. "I don't want to talk with him; you help him," comes the response. The Assistant stares at the phone puzzling over what to do next.

This is a telltale signal of a sales practice bogged down with too many clients of all shapes and sizes; with the Team, in this case a Sales Assistant and a Rookie Junior Partner, left alone to handle the vast array of client issues while the Senior Financial Advisor is unavailable.

**can cover for each other, help each other, and
t ourselves as a Team."**

fer to as a "collective grouping." It's usually done for
...ong reasons. For some it's the convenience of covering for each other when on vacation. For others it's the idea of sharing the expense of support staff. It's also promoted as a marketing strategy, with the hope that Team selling will assist them in closing larger accounts. There are even Financial Advisors who sincerely intend to function as a Team but cannot seem to integrate their efforts. They continue as individuals, selling and handling clients in the same one-dimensional manner as before. They do help each other occasionally, keeping the idea of "Team" alive. Here are the kinds of situations that arise.

- A client of Financial Advisor "A" calls. Since "A" is out, the Sales Assistant transfers the call to Financial Advisor "B". Because the call was for advice on whether or not to purchase a particular stock that "B" was not familiar with, fifteen minutes were wasted. Advisor "A" is left with a message to contact this client regarding the request for advice. Financial Advisor "A" gets this message and blows-up at the Sales Assistant, "You've gotta get this guy to stop calling me. Get "B" to buy whatever he wants, or get licensed so you can make the trade yourself."

- In preparation for a meeting with a fairly substantial prospect, total chaos ensues as they try to pull collateral materials together. For at the same time, they are also scrambling to develop another proposal. It's not simply a matter of selecting an investment product or approach. These new prospects have both expressed multiple financial needs. So, everything comes to a halt while Financial Advisor "A", Financial Advisor "B", and their Sales Assistant anxiously try to figure out what and how to pull it all together. All three can be heard grumbling, "This is not what teamwork is supposed to be like."

Level 2 Teams like the idea of being a Team but are not always willing to learn how to function effectively as a cohesive unit. Typically they are a collection of financial salespeople pretending to function as a Wealth Management Team. The danger lies in their experience as intangibles salespeople, regardless of how skilled they are. Those skills will be a lost cause when it comes to Affluent Investors – they're too savvy. But to themselves, their managers, their firms, and their peers, the perception is that these groups of Financial Advisors just need to get better at what they have been doing. Yet as a Team, they have no written business plan, no clear strategy targeting the affluent, and no thoughts about reducing the large number of clients built up in their individual practices.

Level 3: "The company wants us to form a Team."

This is a big mistake, but it happens a lot. It stems partly from the very issues we addressed at the beginning of this chapter. It takes a Team to meet the multidimensional financial needs of Affluent Investors. However, Teams formed by company mandate are frequently doomed from the start. You need to have your own reasons, which must be shared by every Team Member. Even then, you will have to work very hard to make it work.

Forming a Team does not a Team make. You're bringing together a group of individuals who are used to working independently. Working alone feels good to them; that's one of the reasons they became financial professionals in the first place. So, instead of becoming a *Team* in the true sense of the word, they look for ways to improve *team-work*. They still *focus on individual performance*, but combine it with efforts to share information, ideas, and insights. Closely guarding each individual's turf, they limit decision making to only those things that enable each individual to do their job better. They even attend some Team training, but they leave most of what is presented in the training room, and return to their office to continue business as usual.

Soon they discover that "being a Team" simply adds busy work to their already full schedule. Most important, they know in their heart of hearts that they are not progressing toward becoming an effective Wealth Management Team. At this point they disband (if permitted), continue maintaining the pretense of being a Team, or sit down with some expert help and get serious about moving on to Level 4.

Level 4: "Let's get serious about becoming a legitimate Wealth Management Team."

Despite the effort to become a Team at Levels 2 and 3, the emphasis remains on individual performance functioning within the old sales and marketing model of Wall Street. Level 4 Teams are challenged with functioning in the aftermath of either an arranged (management initiated) or a shotgun (everybody's doing it) marriage. In becoming a Level 4 Team, that all changes. The *focus at Level 4 is on collective performance*, guided by a long-range plan and shaped by a *Metrics Scorecard System*, a common disciplined approach to decision-making, and mutual accountability that is linked to developing a wealth management business. There is no other way to build a successful Team-based *21st Century Financial Practice™*. The specifics of building a Wealth Management Team will be covered in detail throughout Chapters 3 through 14 as you explore the specifics of the *Business Development, Financial Advisory, Operational Efficiency,* and *Client*

Loyalty Processes. The sooner you initiate your efforts to building a Level 4 Wealth Management Team, the better.

Here's my *Tip of the Century.*

If you will start immediately to build a legitimate Level 4 Wealth Management Team while most of your competitors (and those people in your own company and branch office) are still caught struggling with Level 1, 2 or 3; you will gain a competitive advantage that will be difficult, if not impossible, for others to match. That's because your Level 4 Wealth Management Team is totally focused on providing Ritz-Carlton level service to your clients with FedEx efficiency within the context of running a true financial consulting business.

Wealth Management Team Models

We have established that Affluent Investors want a *solutions provider* who can guide and advise them in the multidimensional aspects of their personal finances. We listed 15 typical solutions at the beginning of this chapter.

In Chapter 7, those solutions will be consolidated into 8 Key Financial Advisory Categories. At that point, you will have an opportunity to explore the steps you need to take so that you can provide competent solutions in each category you plan to offer. That will include expanding your Wealth Management Team through a variety of means – hiring, contracting, partnering, etc.

But first, you need to identify the core members of your Wealth Management Team and begin your Team Building process. To help you select the right Team structure, here are four *models* that represent the core Team

Member relationships we have observed and helped to organize over the past 15 years.

1. **Vertical Team – Model One**: Senior Team Member, Rookie Junior Team Member, Parabroker(s) / Para Advisor(s) / Sales Assistant(s) and Specialist(s).

   With this model, the Senior Team Member remains in charge and controls the entire business. The composition of the Team depends upon the corresponding growth and needs of the business, as determined by the Senior Team Member. Other Support Personnel many also be added.

   When this Wealth Management Team begins experiencing success and it is evident the current Team Members are contributing and working well together, it's not unusual for the Senior Team Member to begin relinquishing control and Team Shares to the Junior Team Member and other valuable Team Members.

2. **Vertical Team – Model Two**: Senior Team Member, Experienced Junior Team Member, Parabroker(s) / Para Advisor(s) / Sales Assistant(s) and Specialist(s).

   Similar to *Model One*, this vertical model also has the Senior Team Member in charge of the entire business. And again, the composition of the Team depends upon the corresponding growth and needs of the business as determined by the Senior Team Member.

   Unlike *Model One*, the Junior Team Member is experienced and has developed a personal book of business that is smaller than the Senior Team Member's business.

As this Wealth Management Team experiences success, it's common for the Senior Team Member to reward other Team Members with Team Shares in direct proportion to their performance.

3. **Vertical Team – Model Three**: Senior Team Member, Parabroker(s) / Para Advisor(s) / Sales Assistant(s) and/or Specialist(s).

Within this vertical model, the Senior Team Member is the only official Financial Advisor on the Team. The number of Para Advisors and Specialists will be determined by the scope and growth of the Senior Team Member's business.

It's not unusual for a Para Advisor (former Sales Assistant or clerical person) to be a CFP and be responsible for the financial planning for clients, while another might serve in a more operational role. A Specialist might work with clients in such areas as insurance, estate planning, or taxes.

Similar to the other vertical models, when the Team begins experiencing success and the Para Advisors and/or Specialists become indispensable, Team Shares should be rewarded according to performance and value.

4. **Horizontal Team – Model Four**: Senior Team Member, Senior Team Member and Parabroker(s) / Para Advisor(s) / Sales Assistant(s). Optional: Specialist(s) and/or Junior Team Member (Rookie or Experienced).

This is a Team of equals. Two Senior Financial Advisors decide to merge their respective businesses as equal partners with equal compensation. This has many characteristics of a marriage – the two become one in terms of their business identity. The defining characteristics are similar levels of production and assets. Age and length of service are not critical in the formation of a functional horizontal Team.

After a period of Team success when a discrepancy in age exists, it is not unusual for the senior (in age) to begin thinking in terms of working less, semi-retirement, or even full retirement. This requires a redistribution of Team Shares and a corresponding restructuring of individual Areas of Responsibility.

In the mind of many financial professionals, Goldman Sachs was a leader in establishing the precedent for Teams. In talking with a senior person at Goldman, I was told, "We were way ahead of everybody else on the street when it came to Teams and affluence. But now everybody is focused on working with the affluent and feverishly putting together Teams, so we need to take it to another level."

At the time of our conversation, the average Team at Goldman Sachs was composed of 2.3 Investment Executives and a support staff. Since then I've been told that they have now determined that their most successful Teams have four Investment Executives. As interesting as that fact might be, what is most important to remember is that the growing efforts to develop Wealth Management Teams has gotten their attention. They can feel an increased level of competition knocking at their door.

Once your Wealth Management Team is formed, the challenging and absolutely necessary work of *Team Building* begins. Your first step will be to envision your future and develop a written 5-Year Business Plan. That will be the focus of Chapter 3.

There are other areas that require your attention as well. The following commandments, drawn from our recent research as well as our involvement with more than 600 Teams during the past 15 years, will help you focus your efforts in the right direction. As you read them, note how they relate specifically to a Wealth Management Team targeting Affluent Investor clients.

12* Commandments
of Successful Wealth Management Teams
*Baker's Dozen

1. **Properly Conceived**: You must know exactly why the Team was formed, what each Team Member brings to the table, and how you envision blending your collective experience and expertise to meet the multidimensional needs of affluent clients. There also must be no hidden agendas. Affluent clients don't want a sales group posturing as a Wealth Management Team!

2. **Written Business Plan**: This goes beyond production numbers. Only 43% of the Financial Advisory Teams in our latest survey had a long-range business plan. In fact, only 41% of surveyed Financial Planners reported having a written business plan for their own business. Don't you make that mistake! Business plans draw the entire Team toward one agreed-upon future state. You will learn how to develop that plan in Chapter 3.

3. **Delegated Areas of Responsibility**: As we saw with Team Level 1, assigning daily "urgent" tasks to Sales Assistants will block any possibility of building an effective Team. Each Team Member needs clearly delegated Areas of Responsibility, all focused on providing Ritz-Carlton service with FedEx efficiency. Ambiguity leads to inefficiency and confusion, and you can't afford either

when dealing with Affluent Investors. This will be covered in Chapters 9 and 10.

4. **Total Integrity**: This should go without saying. Your best business plan will blow-up if there is any breach of integrity. Affluent clients want to know they can trust you without exception.

5. **Solid Work Ethic**: This is a gripe we encounter too often with established Teams. In most cases, it stems from having skipped at least two of the first four commandments – and especially from failing to delegate Areas of Responsibility. Disparity in work ethic will ruin a Team. Everyone must do their fair share.

6. **Team Leader**: No Team will thrive without an effective leader. All of the research on Teams in every business setting points to leadership as the most critical success factor. This is especially challenging with horizontal Teams (a Team of equals). Pick a leader – the right leader. It can be a revolving position, but every Team needs definitive leadership.

7. **Single Production Number**: Having everyone pull together to establish a single production number is the best way to avoid conflict of interest. It's almost impossible to create the necessary Team synergy while serving two masters.

8. **Total Accountability**: A well-defined plan is important, but without accountability for all parties involved, including the Senior Team Member, the "plan" is rarely

achieved. We've witnessed Teams divorce over this issue alone.

9. **Team Shares**: Equity ownership plays a powerful role in fueling 110% commitment from every member of your Team. Few things are as powerful as pride of ownership.

10. **Good Communication**: Open, honest and constructive communication will improve every aspect of your Team. Weekly meetings, daily huddles, and planning sessions can contribute to Team growth. If poorly planned and led, they can become a roadblock to Team progress. This goes back to Commandment 6.

11. **Healthy Growth**: As with any living organism, Teams are either growing or dying. There is no in-between. Without growth, any synergy you've created will erode. Without that synergy, your ability to serve clients will soon be lost.

12. **Likability**: You don't need to be best of friends, but you'd better respect each other and work hard to get along. Moodiness, jealousies, etc. create unnecessary problems that can quickly reach the point of no return.

13. **Team Agreement**: A true business needs a Team Agreement covering the basic future contingencies: death, dissolution of Team, additional Team Members, dispute resolution, etc. It can save you both heartaches and money.

Every point listed above requires the effort of every Team Member. How many people does it take to destroy a Team? Only one. If that one person is determined to undermine the Team's efforts, is there anything anyone can do to turn them around? Probably not. Therefore, be urgently patient as you work to develop your *21st Century Financial Practice™* and Wealth Management Team. Too many Teams fail for no other reason than that they were hastily conceived. Everyone assumed the others had similar needs, wants and objectives. Never assume!

When your Wealth Management Team has been formed and you believe everything is going fine, that's when you become most vulnerable. These commandments can help you avoid that. Meet at least once a month for the sole purpose of using these commandments to benchmark how well everyone believes your Team is doing. Keep reminding your Team Members that collectively they are the means to a very important end. That "end" is attracting Affluent Investors and transforming them into loyal clients.

Many Teams fool themselves and attempt to build a wealth management practice on top of their existing sales practice. That is analogous to trying to build a Ritz-Carlton on top of a Red Roof Inn. The ultimate measure of your Team's success is getting the right people, doing the right things, for the right reasons–attracting and servicing Affluent Investors.

The
Business Development Process

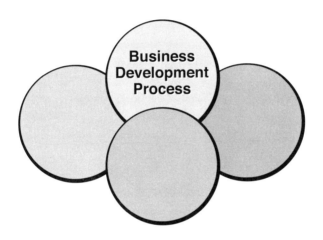

Envisioning
Your Future

The empires of the future
are empires of the mind.

Winston Churchill

Is it important to have a long-range business plan? Ask any highly successful businessperson that question and they will likely say, "Of course." Then ask if they have a written business plan, and again they will likely say, "Of course." Ask whether they refer to it frequently and use it to guide their weekly activities, and once more they will likely say, "Of course."

Ask a typical Financial Advisor and they will likely say, "Yes, it's important – but no, I don't have a written long-range plan." Some will add, "I keep my goals in my head."

Our research within the financial services industry confirms how widespread that "Yes – but no" perspective has become. From a sampling of 2,700 Financial Advisors, 93% of whom are targeting Affluent Investors, only 23% reported having a long-range business plan that goes beyond one-dimensional production goals. In the Observer Stat Bank column of the April 2001 issue of the *Journal of Financial Planning*, it was reported that only 41% of Financial Planners have a written plan for their own business and there's a reason for this.

When you are essentially working alone and your only business development concern is meeting a production (commission) goal, it's perfectly understandable that you would not want to take the time to write out a formal business plan, especially a 5-year plan. That doesn't mean you don't pause now and then to take stock of where you are and think about where you would like to be three to five years down the road. Striving toward goals, thinking about what might be, is the way many financial professionals envision their future. But things are changing, and building a successful *21st Century Financial Practice™* requires taking a different approach.

The Concept of Contextual Pull

Becoming a *successful* Wealth Management Team requires carving out a unique Team identity. That can't happen if you are guided by a collection of individual production goals and dreams. In addition, you form your Wealth Management Team so you can expand the scope of your services to provide solutions for the multidimensional financial needs of Affluent Investors. It's clear that envisioning your future must become a collective effort.

The long-range plan for your Wealth Management Team, needs to serve two important purposes:

- **First**, *it must define the context within which Team goals and all Team activity will take place.* Your plan must be able to provide the answer whenever anyone asks, "Why are we doing this?" It must answer the question, "What do we need?" when you begin to define and assign Team Areas of Responsibility in Chapters 9 and 10. In almost any situation you can think of, your long-range plan must be written in such a way that you can clearly distinguish between what is important and what is not.

- **Second**, *it must continually pull you toward a level of achievement that is clear and exciting to everyone on the Team.* Your plan must clearly show the gap between where you are now and where you want to be as a Team in five years. It must include all the measurements that you use to define success – both qualitative and quantitative.

The combination of these two principles is what we call *contextual pull*. Yogi Berra once commented that, "If you don't know where you are going, you might end up somewhere else." A 5-Year Business Plan that has strong contextual pull has every Team Member saying, "I know exactly where we are going, and I have no doubt that we will get there."

*This is precisely the glue that enabled Alan, Jim, and Mark, three extremely successful Financial Advisors working at a wirehouse, to join forces under the umbrella of a **21st Century Financial Practice**™ and create a Wealth Management Team. All were sole practitioners who had developed successful one-dimensional sales practices that left them with too many total clients, and not enough who would qualify as affluent. After three weeks of collaboration, inventory analysis, and brainstorming, they had roughed out enough of a long- range business plan to review it with me on a conference call.*

"We put a lot of work into this," said Mark. "We're still not sure everything fits, so we're desperate for your feedback. But at least we're in agreement about where we want to take our business as a Team. We want to raise the bar and cater only to wealth, people with five to ten million dollars of investable assets."

*An hour and a half later, the four of us finally concluded our conference call. Out of that call came a 5-Year Business Plan and a **21st Century Metrics System** (Chapter 5) that was unlike anything they had ever created before. As basic* *as all this might appear on the surface, it would not have happened without the intense desire by all three to envision a common future and then transpose this shared vision into a written business plan. Talk about being stretched outside your comfort zone! Each of them confessed that they had never been so thorough or professional in their planning. Yet, all were producing well in excess of a million dollars as financial salespeople.*

Go For Broke

When faced with writing a personal 5-Year Business Plan, most of us will tend toward conservative decisions. However, the research on high achievers shows clearly that they prefer to set stretch goals for which they know they must give 110% in order to have any chance of success. Within Teams, some members may not be as naturally willing to stretch, while others might push harder to take greater risks. Since no one individual is responsible for the results of the Team, it is essential that everyone "go for broke" – commit to a 5-Year Business Plan that forces everyone to stretch. It became obvious during the aforementioned conference call that Alan was being pulled along by Mark and Jim. Dealing exclusively with Affluent Investors was extremely uncomfortable for Alan. However, the support of a Team and the structure of a written plan relieved much of his tension without compromising any aspect of their envisioned future.

To relieve the tension between "hold back" vs "go for broke," there is a tendency for Team Members to compromise, to call for a "middle of the road" plan. This is dead wrong. Instead, you must eliminate the tension altogether by taking the guesswork out of long-range planning and working together as a Team to establish targets you all agree are lofty, but believable and achievable. You still need to "go for broke," not in establishing targets that really stretch you, but in getting your entire Wealth Management Team behind the plan, making certain that it has strong contextual pull.

Four Wealth Management Team Models were described in Chapter 2. Three are Vertical Team Models where the Senior Team Member is "in charge of the entire business." Does that mean the Senior Team Member should develop his or her personal 5-Year Business Plan and then present it to the other Team Members? That's one possibility, but not the only one.

Five years is a long stretch, and your plan will include significantly expanding the financial services and solutions you offer to clients. That developmental process needs to begin now, and that includes inviting people to join your Team who can grow and develop with you. You could develop your plan and then recruit people who have the potential and desire to help you get there. On the other hand, you might prefer to pull together a core group of people following one of the Vertical Models, and then have them join you in developing a Team 5-Year Business Plan.

With the Horizontal Team Model, it's vital that at least the Senior Team Members work together on the plan. But here again, you might decide to pull other core people in and include them in the planning process. In the case of Alan, Jim, and Mark, their support personnel were not engaged in the initial phase of creating their 5-Year Business Plan. They felt it was important that they first discover what it would take for them to create a common vision and learn to work well together and I agreed.

Creating Your 5-Year Business Plan

The typical way to create a 5-Year Business Plan is to simply define the results or outcomes you want to achieve at the end of that time period. However, plans created that way are the ones that usually sit on the shelf and gather dust. Since those outcomes don't have to be accomplished for five years, it's difficult to see what will be gained by looking at the plan.

MBA schools abound with templates for creating a business plan. The problem is that very few of the professors espousing these complex instruments have ever built a profitable business. As a result, they get carried away in the academic and theoretical busywork. But most entrepreneurs are able to create their business plan out of a vision, seeing something that is not there, believing in it without proof, and developing a simple working plan to make it happen. The result is a plan fueled by total commitment to the long-range strategy, but inherently flexible in the day-to-day working tactics.

The process begins with what I refer to as the "crystal ball" exercise. Imagine looking into a crystal ball and envisioning your *21st Century Financial Practice™* five years from today. Imagine the exact profile of the clientele you would like to be serving. Visualize the solutions and value you will be providing for the multidimensional aspects of their personal finances. Dream of the amount of assets you will be managing and the revenue you will generate. Visualize your quality of life in the theatre of your mind. From this trip down fantasy lane, you will prepare yourself for developing a functional long-range business plan.

The effort to achieve a plan, any plan, involves closing the gap between where you are now and the results you want to achieve. Stating what you want to achieve is relatively easy. Closing that "where we are to where we want to be" gap is the real challenge; and that's where your Team needs to focus their attention and energy, just as soon as your plan is completed. The plan must be stated in such a way that it will facilitate that "*closing the gap*" process.

The best way to ensure that this will happen is to create your 5-Year Business Plan by following these steps.

1. Select the specific *categories* to use in building your plan. Here are our suggestions:

   - Total number of clients and households.

   - Distribution of clients by income and wealth to clearly distinguish between those in affluent categories from those less than affluent.

   - Profile of your Ideal Client (income, net worth, circles of influence, etc.).

   - Financials: assets under management, annual production, sources of income (fees vs commissions), personal income, etc.

   - Wealth Management Team makeup plus utilization of Senior/Junior Team Members, Specialists, and Support people.

   - Business development strategy: how you attract, qualify, and close prospective clients.

   - Quality of your personal life: this should be a personal addendum for each Team Member.

2. Analyze and document *where you are now* in each of those categories, even if the answer is, "We haven't done anything as yet." Provide specific and comprehensive information for each category.

3. Project each category out five years and clearly define the *changes you want to see in place at that point in time*. Take the specific "where you are now" information from each category and then describe (specifically and comprehensively) the changes you want to occur.

   Achieving your 5-Year Business Plan will actually take you through two phases of development:

- **Phase 1**: From our experience with coaching Wealth Management Teams through this transition, it will take you 18 months to 2 years to work your way through the four processes described in this book and establish your *21st Century Financial Practice™*. At that point, your *Business Development, Financial Advisory, Operational Efficiency,* and *Client Loyalty Processes* should be in place.

- **Phase 2**: It will take you another 2 to 3 years to strategically position yourselves in each of the Affluent Investor Target Markets you select (see Chapter 6) and actually achieve a competitive advantage in those markets. That means two things.

  - First, you have a well established network and referral system within those target markets and are providing a consistent level of service and efficiency that gives you an advantage over current competitors.

  - Second, you are so well established and continually working so hard to improve, that it is literally impossible for others to enter those market segments and compete successfully with you.

The "changes you want to have in place" portion of your 5-Year Business Plan needs to focus on Phase 2, not Phase 1. Phase 1 is your first incremental step, but Phase 2 is the outcome you should be experiencing within five years. You will have an opportunity to address Phase 1 elements when you develop your *21st Century Metrics System* in Chapter 5.

When you create a 5-Year Business Plan in these terms, the focus of your ongoing thinking, discussions and actions can be toward closing the gap. When the plan has been drafted, meet as a Team and ask these questions: "Now that we have drawn up our 5-Year Business Plan, is closing the gap we have created going to stretch us, force us to grow? At the same time, is it both realistic and achievable?"

What you will be evaluating is the journey you will take, not just the destination you hope to reach. As you go through the plan category by category, keep asking the questions for each one and make any adjustments you all agree should be made. If you disagree, encourage everyone to keep talking about it until you can reach a *consensus*.

Consensus does not mean that everyone has to agree. It does mean that everyone feels they have an ample opportunity to express their opinions – and that they either agree or are willing to accept the decision, and willfully support it.

Many Financial Advisors elect to skip this step. As critical as this step is in developing a functional Wealth Management Team, some veteran Financial Advisors have a tendency to groan when forced to complete this exercise. I've heard, "Come on Matt! We know about the importance of business planning and we'll get to it – someday. Just show us how to get more affluent clients."

Beware! If you cannot make time to develop a written 5-Year Business Plan, you will struggle to reach a consensus on many of the salient aspects of developing a successful Wealth Management Team. Basic questions like: "What will be our marketing strategy and tactics?" "How will we delegate Areas of Responsibility?" "Who will be accountable for what?" "Are we being realistic?" will remain unanswered. Over time, these issues will grow into major obstacles. I could go on, but fresh in my mind is the following real-life example.

Three Financial Advisors were anxious to form a Wealth Management Team. Using their best efforts at persuasion, they asked me to agree to an exploratory conference call. However the call didn't go quite the way they expected. It was over in less than ten minutes. Andrew, the most vocal of the three, accused me of sabotaging their efforts because I didn't agree with his initial premise for forming a Team. Ugh! Later in the day, one of the other Financial Advisors called to express his regrets and thanks. Apparently, Andrew was trying to steamroll the others into forming a Team.

At the time of this writing, they are approaching things more businesslike and working hard to reach a consensus. Andrew still doesn't think they need a business plan as a pre-requisite for forming a Team; but he is in the minority. I have no knowledge of the outcome of their efforts but must confess to harboring serious doubts that a true Wealth Management Team will emerge.

When you take the time and expend the energy to reach a total consensus regarding your 5-Year Business Plan, the discussion can become more businesslike and realistic. It will provide a path from which you can shift, from deciding whether the goal you have set is realistic and achievable to determining how to close the gap in the time frame you have set. That on-going discussion will provide the contextual pull you need to be successful.

In the next chapter we will help you create *your Ideal Client Profile*, ensuring that all of your future efforts will be linked to attracting, servicing, and retaining those affluent clients. In Chapter 5 we will introduce the *21st Century Metrics System* that will enable you to measure and monitor the answers you generate from that *"How do we close the gap?"* question.

Creating Your
Ideal Client Profile

Appearances are deceptive.

Aesop

J*ack, a successful stockbroker, had been resting on his laurels for at least three years. With more than 1,000 clients on the books, both he and his licensed assistant Lane were kept very busy. After all, how busy you are is one of the ways we measure success these days, right? Jack wasn't so sure. He was beginning to wonder about a number of things and had some serious questions when I met with him.*

"If I keep pushing our marketing efforts, how will we handle the additional clients? How many are going to be pulled away by the exploding on-line investment information and opportunities, especially now that major investment houses are offering discount-pricing strategies? With over 1,000 clients, it's hard to know what each client is thinking."

"Maybe we'd better step-up our marketing and sales efforts just in case. To do that, I'll need at least one new assistant. Lane is already overworked, but I'm not sure we can afford to expand now. Those 1,000 plus clients aren't generating enough revenue. What is the right strategy for these uncertain, fast changing times?"

Because Wall Street has long been driven by a sales and marketing model, brokers have been trained to think and act like salespeople. Despite Jack's years of experience, you can clearly hear this influence in his comments and questions. That also helps to explain why our research revealed that so many service and support needs are falling through the cracks. No matter how knowledgeable a support person is, there is a limit to the number of clients a two person Team can adequately serve at a value based relationship level.

We all know that sales and marketing efforts are the means to a specific end. The real problem lies with that end. The old sales and marketing model encourages brokers to simply "collect clients." Jack, with Lane's able assistance, had done exactly that. They assumed that the most successful brokers are those who collect the most clients. "One investor at a time" may be good advertising, but it's a myth, and always has been. The real battle cry has been "as many clients as possible!"

The irony is that when trying to attract, service, and retain Affluent Investor clients, "one investor at a time" moves from myth to absolute necessity. That necessity results in the need to formulate a systematic *Financial Advisory Process* that will address the multidimensional financial needs of your clients (see Chapter 8). Making that transition smoothly and effectively begins with creating your *Ideal Client Profile*.

I asked Jack and Lane how many of their 1,000 "client collection" could be categorized as Affluent Investors, those whose yearly income is $135,000 or more. As you might guess, they weren't quite sure. They couldn't even be certain that they had identified the yearly income of all their clients. At the same time, they readily admitted that Affluent Investors are the most desirable clients. That was the turning point. They began to make that all-important paradigm shift from *collecting* the "most clients" to *targeting* the "right clients." Sounds a bit scary, doesn't it? It feels much better to add clients than to cut them.

Our research established that 88% of Affluent Investors employed the services of a financial professional and that 90% did not use the Internet for serious financial decisions. Our research also demonstrated that to gain and maintain client loyalty, you must meet and even exceed their expectations, and do so on an ongoing, long-term basis. There is no way you can do that if you have too many clients and cannot identify your Affluent Investor client base.

> *"I've categorized all my clients," complained Mitch, another Financial Advisor working to make the change. "I don't understand why this step is so important." After much discussion, and at my insistence, Mitch agreed to allow two weeks to complete our **Net Profit Contribution Analysis** and (along with his Assistant) conduct a client activity analysis study. After two weeks of work, what he discovered shocked him.*
>
> - *92% of his business was coming from 12% of his 836 clients,*
>
> - *65% of his and his Assistant's time was devoted to serving the 88% of his clients that were bringing in only 8% of his revenue.*

That is the sales and marketing approach in action; and, needless to say, it got Mitch's attention. Did it get your attention? If so, the following steps will help you to create your *Ideal Client Profile*.

Step One: Analyze Your Client Base

First you must closely analyze your current *client base*. How many clients do you have? Which can be considered as truly profitable? Which can you upgrade by establishing a value based professional relationship with them? How can you move from simply collecting clients to building a profitable, growing *21st Century Financial Practice™?*

We refer to this as a *Net Profit Contribution Analysis*. The objective is to identify those clients who should be the target of your efforts. Instead of trying to manage "a cast of thousands," you will grow your business in the right direction by first focusing on your *Top 25 Net Profit Contribution Clients*. These are the present clients who meet any of the following criteria.

Net Profit Contribution Criteria:

- The highest level of total assets on your books.

- The highest level of gross commissions/fees generated over the past 12 months.

- Has the potential for more assets and/or more gross commissions/fees in the next 12 months that would be comparable to the first two criteria – or higher.

- Has a strong enough center of influence – and you have a strong enough relationship with them – that they would be willing to introduce or refer you to others, who have a potential for assets and/or gross commissions/fees during the next 12 months, that would be comparable to your best net profit contribution clients (or higher).

You will need a list of all your clients and access to each client file. As you study each client's file, place a big star (*) in front of their name on the list *if* they meet one or more of the above four criteria. Once you have gone through your entire list, go back over those you have starred (*) and narrow down that list to your top 25. Make a new list of those 25, and title it your "*Top 25 Net Profit Contribution Clients.*"

If you are in the process of building your Team or already have a Wealth Management Team in place, be certain you involve them in this process. Don't wait until Step Two and then spring it on them.

This is a torturous process for most financial professionals. It takes time, and it will push you way beyond your present comfort zone. As one individual said, "I understand the need to go from *quantity* to *quality*, but I'm uneasy about trying to make the switch." Let's face it, the sales and marketing game is fueled by a false security in numbers. But exceeding the expectations of Affluent Investors is a different game in every way. Without this false sense of security, you will be forced to deliver the goods in all aspects of your value based professional relationship. And for most financial professionals, this requires substantial retooling. Put simply, it means change.

Step Two: Analyze Your Client Activity

In his classic article, *What Is Strategy*, Harvard Business Professor Michael Porter points out that the best companies define their *strategic positioning* in terms of the *value* provided to their customers. He writes,

> Competitive strategy is about being different. It means deliberately choosing a different set of activities to deliver a unique mix of value.

"Deliberately choosing a different set of activities" is an important thread woven throughout this entire book. Your *Top 25 Net Profit Contribution Clients* list represents your greatest source of present business and the launching pad for upgrading to Affluent Investors in the future. The question is this, are these clients currently receiving the attention required to maximize that potential?

You will need to bring your current Team together and have everyone (no exceptions) maintain a *Client Contact Time and Activity Log* for the next two weeks. Each client contact made, whether by phone, fax, e-mail, or in-person, must be recorded with the following information.

- *Date* and *time* of the contact.

- *Who* on the Team was contacted.

- *Nature* of the contact.

- *Length* of time for the contact.

- *Time required to satisfy the client.*

> *Jack and Lane were open to Step One and did a good job of applying the Net Profit Contribution Criteria to their 1,000 plus clients. Lane, however, was not enthusiastic about conducting a two week time and activity analysis of client contacts. "I know where we waste time. This is simply more busywork," was her position. But Jack and I persisted, and Jack promised to keep a log as well.*
>
> *Two weeks later, Lane reported that over 85% of her time had been spent on clients who were not generating much, if any, revenue. Up to that point, they had been in denial, operating a discount financial sales practice but trying to convince themselves that they were The Bessemer Trust Company.*

Guesswork will not work here. Everyone we have worked with, who guessed ahead of time, was shocked two weeks later. Do the work and you will be pleased that you did. Not only will the results tell you who gets your time and effort, but you will also uncover valuable information about the kinds of contacts that are initiated by you, your Team Members and your clients.

Step Three: Create Your Ideal Client Profile

In Chapter 1, we indicated that there was a potential market of 16,300,000 households with a net worth of $500,000 plus. That's not bad, especially when it continues to grow as it has (22% in one five year period). That's comforting, but the question remains: How do *you* attract the Affluent Investors? The anxiety behind that question usually stems from two factors.

- Looking at an overwhelming number (16 million plus) without knowing where to begin and how to truly reach them.

- Feeling somewhat intimidated about entering the haunts of the very wealthy.

The process of creating your *Ideal Client Profile* is designed to help you address each of these concerns and overcome any reluctance you may have about "moving up" to that market. We will break that market down into manageable chunks, enabling you to make clear choices about whom you want to target. With that information, you will be able to create your *Ideal Client Profile* – your first step toward ensuring that your 5-Year Business Plan becomes a reality.

One of the decisions you will be making is where to *target* your business development efforts. The higher you focus up the income and wealth ladder, the more challenging it will be to meet the expectations and needs of your clients. However, those upper income levels are experiencing dramatic growth. The *Map of Money and Position* published by Forbes magazine in October of 1999 and shown on the following page, describes the recognized categories of wealth at that time.

Your first commitment as a Team is to "reach up" – to place an imaginary *firewall* no lower than the Upper-Middle Class category, and possibly at the Rich (Semi-Affluent) category. Once you put that firewall in place, you need to reach the point where you can commit to staying above it. You will be able to do that when you have done the following:

- Developed a strategy for reaching the Affluent Investor Market Segments you select, which will be addressed in Chapter 6.

- Determined the disposition of those current clients who are in the categories below your firewall. This is critical, because you soon will be too busy with your new marketing strategy to adequately service those clients. At the same time, you will want to do this in a way in which they will receive the level of attention they need.

Map of Money and Position		
Category	**Income**	**Wealth**
Superrich *(Affluent)*	$10 million plus	$100 million plus
Rich *(Semi-Affluent)*	$1 to $10 million	$10 to $100 million
Upper-Middle Class *(Targeted by our study)*	$75,000 to $1 million	$500,000 to $10 million
Middle Class	$35,000 to $75,000	$55,000 to $500,000
Lower-Middle Class	$15,000 to $35,000	$10,000 to $55,000
Poor	$0 to $15,000	$0 to $10,000

Note: We included the *Affluent* and *Semi-Affluent* labels in parentheses because several people writing about Affluent Investors use them. Our initial research focused on investors with an average annual income of $135,000, which places them in the Forbes Upper-Middle Class category.

Now you are ready to target specific segments of the Affluent Investor market. We have found that a very effective way to accomplish that is to categorize them on the *basis of how they achieved their wealth.*

- *Generators* **of Wealth**. Achieved their wealth through their own enterprise as opposed to earning it or receiving it from another source.

- *Earners* **of Wealth**. Achieved their wealth as employees.

- *Receivers* **of Wealth**. Received their wealth through retirement, stock options, divorce, or inheritance.

- *Managers* **of Wealth**. These individuals usually are not wealthy, but they do manage the wealth of their organizations.

As you read through these brief descriptions, think of the *Top 25 Net Profit Contribution Clients* you identified and of the people that you and other Team Members know, whose financial situation places them above the firewall you established. You will probably see some links to one or more of these categories and you should make note of those links.

As we further break down each of these categories, basic opportunities and challenges will be noted. Your Team should go through these descriptions together and identify those *segments* of the above categories that are likely *targets* in your effort to successfully attract Affluent Investor clients. As you go through these descriptions, evaluate them using the following criteria:

- The background of each Team Member – where each one has worked, and the knowledge and associations of each that provide links to specific segments.

- Your circles of influence – clients, family, friends, acquaintances, etc.

- Your collective areas of specialty – the financial areas you know best and the solutions you are presently equipped to provide.

- Specific clients and others you know that are "members" of a given segment.

With that in mind, review the following Affluent Investor Market Segments and place check marks (✓) where you see possibilities.

Generators of Wealth

☐**Entrepreneurs** – their income and net worth varies significantly. The top 10% dominate the market. Look for entrepreneurs who have been successful at creating a growing business, who have been in business at least 10 years, and are 50 years or older. Even though not technically "start-ups," franchise owners can also be a possibility.

- Segment further by industry, but look especially for growth industries in growth markets.

☐**Self-employed Professionals** (medical professionals, attorneys, consultants, engineers, airline pilots, architects, coaches, chefs, etc.) – their business typically has little value when it is time to retire, so they need to establish and wisely fund their own retirement plans rather than depend on selling their business.

- Segment further by profession, professional accreditation, and area of specialty.

☐**Artists and Entertainers** – some make huge incomes, and others make a good and steady living. Their agents tend to act as gatekeepers, making them hard to reach. Many of the younger prospects have flamboyant and unstable lifestyles.

- Segment further by type of artist/entertainer, by geographic centers such as Los Angeles, New York or Nashville, or by fast-rising vs stable.

☐**Professional Athletes** – the numbers involved and the salaries many are paid make this a fast growing industry. The serious money, however, comes from product endorsements, etc. A big challenge is the young age and short length of most athletic careers. You also have to deal with agents, lawyers, and managers who act as gatekeepers. In fact, they are often the only doorway to the athlete.

- Segment further by sport and by geographic location.

Earners **of Wealth**

☐**Key Corporate Employees** (executives, managers, professionals, and skilled technicians) – since they are usually taken care of by their company, the best time to approach these folks is when they are changing jobs or about to retire. The biggest opportunity is with those who, in addition to their retirement plan, own stock options in fast growth companies.

- Segment further by industry, specialty, professional accreditation, or the designations above in parentheses.

☐**Salespeople** (essentially those on commission) – they are often overlooked by Financial Planners, yet the best earn well over $100,000 a year.

- Segment further by specific industry.

Receivers of Wealth

☐**Retirees** – approximately 33 million baby boomers will soon retire, adding to the 30 million currently over age 65. Many retirees are struggling financially, yet there are many others that represent a very profitable target for Financial Advisors.

- Segment further by focusing on retirement communities in warmer climates. When people move there, they are often open to *being introduced* to a Financial Advisor (but not to a traditional "sales pitch"). Another approach is to focus on companies with strong retirement plans and/or stock options, local union chapters, outplacement services or on retired employee networks.

☐**Divorced Women** – about 1.2 million divorces occur each year. In the top 5 to 10 percent of the most financially successful marriages, the wife typically gets all the liquid assets and the house, leaving the business related assets to her husband.

A spouse in this situation is often called "out spouse" because their support comes primarily from *his* attorney, accountant, investment advisor, and insurance agent. This provides a wide-open opportunity to help the former wife who has all those assets, but no personal advisor.

☐**Widows** – women live an average of seven years longer than their husband. Over 650,000 women are widowed yearly and, in many cases, they must suddenly take over all that financial stuff. Often their goal is to simplify everything, consolidate and get their wills and estate plans in order. Estate planning attorneys are good doorways to this segment.

☐**Inheritors** – the largest transfer of generational wealth ever will take place in the next 20 years (between $10 to $15 trillion in assets). It's especially important to build relationships with the children of the people you are advising, especially those children who are over age 50. Estate planning professionals are good doorways to this segment as well.

Managers of Wealth

☐**Qualified Retirement Plans** – this market has insurance and retirement plan needs but the competition is fierce. Because cost becomes a leverage tool, margins are typically small. With capital-intensive companies, their assets are basically real estate, equipment, and inventory. Knowledge based companies are more labor-intensive, and some employees are very well paid.

- You will need to find very specialized segments where you can provide specific, highly valued service.

☐**Not-for-profit Organizations** – have budgeted operations which are funded through a variety of sources, ranging from usage fees to large endowments. They typically hire professional management firms and outside consultants. Your best strategy would be to focus on smaller organizations that are well managed and funded. The movers and shakers who tend to serve on their boards could open doors for you.

- Segment further by organizational size. Categories such as educational, health related, associations, etc. would also make viable segments.

☐ **Municipalities** – the dollars are larger and the needs greater than in private markets, but it's important to master the politics of the municipality and enjoy being in the middle of it. They bring in large tax revenues and have a wide variety of financial service needs.

- Segment further by type of municipal department.

☐ **Charities and Foundations** – operational cash flow can be a challenge since it comes from contributions and/or investment returns. Both charities and foundations are often strong on the values that formed them in the first place and trust will be paramount.

- Segment further by size and type.

With your checked segment(s) in mind, you are now ready to create your *Ideal Client Profile*, which involves three levels of decisions.

1. First you must decide which Affluent Investor Market Segment(s) to target, selecting at least one from above – but no more than three.

2. Your second decision refers back to the firewall you established earlier. Look again at those categories, discuss them together, and then select an *ideal* minimum of investable assets you would like to accept when opening an account for a new client. That's the ideal, and you may feel you aren't at the point where you can make that a hard and fast rule. So the next thing to do is select an *interim* minimum level of investable assets that you will use on a temporary basis. Your goal is to incrementally increase that *interim* minimum level until it matches your *ideal*;

so it would be wise to establish target dates for each incremental move you hope to make.

3. Your third and final decision is to list any other criteria you would like to add, that clearly define the Ideal Client for you. Consider the following.

    -   A minimum age.

    -   A minimum amount of discretionary cash flow with which to buy insurance, invest and pay your fees.

    -   Expectations of clients regarding their financial future.

    -   Having a long-term rather than a short-term perspective.

    -   Valuing the services of a competent Wealth Management Team.

    -   Being respected centers of influence that will provide introductions and referrals within their target market segment, or possibly other segments.

Putting forth adequate effort and care into creating your *Ideal Client Profile* will enable you to:

-   Recognize prospective clients as you meet them.

-   Quickly qualify prospects, knowing that you have the right solutions for them and can provide the type of valued services they seek.

-   Successfully establish a long-term Financial Advisory relationship with your clients – especially if you take special care listing the criteria that will define your Ideal Client.

Creating your *Ideal Client Profile* can have a dramatic impact on your future success. When you have a clear picture in your mind of who you want to attract to your business, it's amazing how those people keep appearing in your periscope. They've always been there, but in the past you weren't diligently looking for them. They drifted by in the quiet waters, and you simply didn't see them. Now, you will. Trust me, you will! And as you continue through this book, you'll become equipped to do something about it.

Incidentally

In our late 20th century research with Affluent Investors, we asked them which was more important, their relationship with their financial professional or the firm he or she represented. Seventy percent indicated the individual financial professional. This is cause for celebration – and for caution. It means that your Affluent Investor clients will hold you person-ally accountable for the solutions and service you provide, because *you are their value agenda.*

Developing Your
21st Century Metrics System

On the folly of rewarding A,
while hoping for B
Steve Kerr

Traditional metrics don't force a
company to consider performing against
new and unorthodox competitors.
Gary Hamel

The Wealth Management workshop had barely finished when I was quickly cornered by one of the participants and ushered into a small conference room. What transpired was the initial stage of a major paradigm shift – from simply keeping score to creating a metrics system that would drive performance.

"Look at these numbers," commanded my abductor, "I've always been in the first quintile in every one of my firm's measurements since I've been in the business. Last year I opened 135 new accounts, which placed me in the first quintile for my length of service. If I had focused only on my **Ideal Client Profile** as you suggested, only a handful, if any, would have qualified. Please understand, I'm not an idiot, but I feel like my firm has turned me into one of Pavlov's dogs. The thought

---

of developing my own metrics system is extremely uncomfortable." This was one of those exciting situations where the mind of an intelligent person was starting to pull him beyond his comfort zone.

The irony was that the firm in question, a major wire house and industry leader, thought they were doing everything possible to persuade their distribution force to stop opening accounts with smaller clients and start focusing exclusively on Affluent Investors. However, they had overlooked something critical – their *metrics system.* Their measurements of success did not match their rhetoric, and what a company measures always wins out over what they say.

The good news is that it's easier for a person, or even a Team, to change their score keeping system than it is for a larger organization. Every Wealth Management Team who is part of a larger entity will be able to make this adjustment in it's entirety, sooner than their parent firm. It won't be easy and it won't be comfortable. Why? Because we are creatures of habit as my workshop abductor so clearly demonstrated.

A major contribution from the Quality Movement was the realization that if you want to improve performance, you have to measure it. The collective set of measurements used by an organization became known as their *metrics system.*

By the mid-90's, metrics systems were the talk of the town. However, the talk wasn't always so glowing. In his 1996 book *Keeping Score,* Mark Graham Brown noted that "Most managers and technical professionals spend at least 25% of their time reviewing metrics." He went on to say,

I see a lot of time wasted looking at data that has questionable value to running the organization ... looking at the wrong metrics can confuse decision making and lead to the wrong business decisions.

The traditional metrics system used in the financial services industry has been production – typically measured quarterly and yearly. Financial metrics have serious limitations for measuring performance. They are what Robert Kaplan and David Norton call "lagging indicators", that "tell some, but not all, of the story about past actions", and "fail to provide adequate guidance for the actions to be taken today and the day after to create future financial value."

In *Leading The Revolution,* Gary Hamel points to another metrics problem that is especially relevant in today's business world which he describes as "a world where innovation is the surest route to wealth creation." He emphasizes, "Without strong pro-innovation metrics, the default setting in most organizations is 'more of the same'." *Wealth creation* is the definitive phrase. It's the result you want to bring to your Affluent Investor clients – and in the process, the result your Wealth Management Team must produce for itself and the company that employs it.

Consider this scenario. You established production goals at the beginning of the year. You even broke the numbers down by quarter so you could review them each quarter. Now, at the end of the first quarter, you are checking to see how well you did. You look to see what the numbers *are* – but the real question is, "What do the numbers *mean?*"

As Kaplan and Norton point out, financial measures are based on what has already been done. They tell you nothing about what you *need to do* in the future. You need a metrics system that will indicate how well you are progressing incrementally in your efforts to close the gap defined by your 5-Year Business Plan. We call it a *21st Century Metrics System.* The "21st Century" designation is no gimmick. It's used to emphasize that the old metrics systems of the past will not work here.

Your *21st Century Metrics System* is linked to the following factors necessary for success – the key financial practice development drivers.

- The increased number of Ideal Clients you have attracted; that is *Ideal Clients* not just any clients. Ideal Clients are a primary indicator of your future success. You defined your *Ideal Client Profile* in Chapter 4.

- The number of current clients you have been able to upgrade to Ideal Client status. Again, this is a primary success indicator.

- The number of prospects you have in the pipeline who meet your *Ideal Client Profile* criteria. The rest probably aren't important enough to measure.

- Your Client and Prospective Client contacts are checkpoints and decision points of your system.

- Specifically what you have done to improve the value you bring to your clients – your client value agenda. The emphasis is on what you have done that will add new value in the future.

- The revenue generated from your new and upgraded Ideal Clients, which is a lagging indicator, but still important within the context of your total metrics system.

- The new assets acquired from your new and upgraded Ideal Clients. Assets are your future.

- Net Profit of your Financial Advisory Practice. Not just the amount, but what trends do you see? Does all the above indicate a future growth pattern?

These are what we call *Indicators of Success*. Measuring the factors that *indicate* success is what ultimately will *produce* success. Going back to the beginning of this chapter, it's clear that our *21st Century Metrics*

System meets each criterion established by all three authors we quoted earlier.

- It clarifies decision making and leads to the right business decisions.

- It includes some "lagging indicators" but couples them with other performance indicators that will "tell the story about past actions" and give guidance to future actions.

- It has the pro-innovation emphasis that is required to build a Wealth Management Team that successfully targets Affluent Investors.

Let's go back a moment to your 5-Year Business Plan. The *Indicators of Success* principle sounds good in theory – but old habits are hard to break, especially when they are attitudinal. This brings a recent example to mind.

> *Feeling bored and stuffed from our family Thanksgiving meal, I excused myself from the table and headed for my computer to check my e-mail. Much to my surprise, there was a full-page message from the Senior Partner of a Wealth Management Team I was working with. After apologizing for communicating on Thanksgiving, he went on to raise concerns over the production of his practice being flat and the difficulty he was experiencing repositioning his practice as a wealth management boutique. I responded immediately that he should call my office and set-up a conference call.*
>
> *I was extremely curious as to what would be uncovered during this call. This was a very professional group that was following the steps and appeared to be working diligently toward building a 21st Century Financial Prac-*

tice™. They had established two Ideal Client Profiles, one for the Senior Partner and another for the Junior Partner. I had assisted them in creating a 21st Century Metrics System that included fixed daily activities and Metrics Scorecards. But obviously, there was a problem.

Both partners were on the conference call. I began by asking them to pull out their Metrics Scorecards. From there I proceeded to simply go down each of the items – the new Ideal Client fixed daily activities, upgrade activities, etc. for both of them. It wasn't long until the Senior Partner interrupted by saying, "Matt, we're sitting here looking at each other and are both feeling embarrassed. We should know better. It's obvious that if we simply followed our Metrics Scorecards, our problems would be disappearing, and our business would be in a serious growth mode."

As we discussed the situation in more detail, they confessed to being influenced by several things:

- *Their firm.*

- *Other stockbrokers in their office (they had been very successful brokers at a wire house that still used gross production as the one-dimensional measurement).*

- *The dot-com collapse and subsequent stock market correction.*

Collectively, these influences caused them to fall into the trap of thinking and acting like salespeople. Their focus became commissions (lagging indicators) and they were not following the future success indicators that made up their Metrics Scorecards. This is a major paradigm shift, simple in concept but often challenging to implement.

So how do you begin this paradigm shift? You implement a metrics system that ensures that you are consistently measuring the *important* things that will indicate your progress toward accomplishing your 5-Year Business Plan. You do that by using what we call *Metrics Scorecards*. And you stay on track by reviewing them weekly; a lesson learned by the Team described above.

There are two levels of Metrics Scorecards that you will need to incorporate into your Team activities: *Yearly Metrics Scorecards* as well as *Interim Metrics Scorecards* maintained on a quarterly and weekly basis.

Yearly Metrics Scorecards

You begin by creating your *Yearly Metrics Scorecard (Year One)*, which will consist entirely of *targets* for that first year.

Year One also launches Phase 1 of your 5-Year Business Plan. Your Wealth Management Team should be focused on successfully completing the *four processes* while also maintaining contact with current important clients and attracting others to your practice. It requires a balancing act, and that needs to be reflected in your Yearly Metrics Scorecard. When your Team gathers to create this scorecard, discuss this balance and consider it with each metrics criterion you set. Here is what we suggest you include.

- Begin with the typical financial targets of such things as assets under management, the percent that will be fee-based at that point, production, and gross profits.

- Follow with Ideal Client targets in three categories: Existing Ideal Clients, Upgraded to Ideal Clients and New Ideal Clients. You will establish targets for the number of clients, assets managed, and year's production for *each* category.

- Next, set a target for the number of Ideal Client prospects you will have in the pipeline at the end of the first year. As you focus on Ideal Clients and require a minimum level of investment, the total number of clients you serve will most likely diminish. At the same time, your production and assets will increase because of the affluent clients you serve. The importance of always having Ideal Client prospects in the pipeline will also increase because it may take longer to attract them and take them through the qualification and closing process.

- Finally, write a description of what your client value agenda will look like at that point, particularly including the solutions and services you will be offering that you know will bring true value to your clients

Your next step is to develop similar *Yearly Metrics Scorecards for Years Two, Three, Four, and Five*. Three decisions will be required.

- First, determine increases to project for each of the next four years in order to make your 5-Year Business Plan a reality.

- Second, forecast changes you anticipate in creating equilibrium between getting through the *four processes* of the *21st Century Financial Practice™*, satisfying current clients, and attracting new clients. This is especially important with Year Two as you are completing Phase 1 of your 5-Year Business Plan and beginning to focus on Phase 2.

- Third, anticipate contributions *Existing* Ideal Clients will make toward your asset, production, and profit goals *versus* the contributions that will come from *New* Ideal Clients. As you progress through these years, the *Converted To Ideal*

Client category will probably diminish and ultimately be eliminated.

Yearly Metrics Scorecards focus primarily on results. You also need a more timely way to track those all-important *indicators* of success. This is where Interim Metrics Scorecards come into the picture.

Interim Metrics Scorecards

Interim Metrics Scorecards take a different approach. You begin by establishing *targets* for a set of performance indicators that you believe will tell you whether or not you are on-target with your current yearly scorecard. At the end of the time period, you will enter the *actual results* and compare those metrics with your targets.

Your first Interim Metrics Scorecard will be developed and reviewed on a *quarterly basis.*

At the *beginning* of each quarter, you should establish *targets* for at least the following six key factors:

- New Ideal Clients,

- Current Clients upgraded to Ideal,

- New assets generated,

- Percent of your Ideal Clients that you will retain,

- Total assets plus the percentage that are fee-based, and

- Ideal Client prospects in the pipeline.

At the *end* of the quarter, you record the *actual* numbers and calculate the percentage over or under your target. Finally, you should write an explanation for those items *over* target as well as an explanation of those items *under* target. It's as important to pinpoint the reasons for exceeding a target, as it is to evaluate why you did not achieve it. If you exceed targets frequently, you probably need to establish more challenging targets.

Your second category of Interim Metrics Scorecard will be developed and reviewed on a *weekly basis*. That's right, there are at least five factors you should be tracking each week. These true *indicators* of future *success* should include the following:

- Client review meetings.

- Client upgrade meetings.

- Three Client Contact factors: Introductions, Client referrals, and Alliance referrals – all of which you will learn about in Chapter 6.

At the beginning of the week you should establish *targets* for each. At the end of the week record the *actual* numbers and calculate the percent over or under for each. Finally, you should again explain why you are *over* target or *under* target.

If you view the weekly or any of the other Metrics Scorecards as busy work, they will probably become just that. If you understand the value of measuring key factors that are *indicators* of future *performance success*, you can shape these scorecards so that they become the fuel that drives your *21st Century Financial Practice™*.

When you look back at the numbers you produced over the last year or quarter, it's too late to do anything about them – and financial numbers provide no clues about what to do in the future. When you incorporate *success indicators* into a combined weekly, quarterly, and yearly Metrics Scorecard System, you will know exactly what you have to do at the beginning of each week – which is exactly the right timing to ensure your future success. In time, you may even decide to make adjustments to your 5-Year Business Plan so it is more in line with the rate of progress you have been tracking through your metrics system.

There is one more piece to the metrics system puzzle – Fixed Daily Activities.

Fixed Daily Activities

Here's where we get down to the nitty-gritty, day-to-day stuff! There are certain tasks that need to be done consistently on a daily, weekly, monthly, and/or quarterly basis to ensure that your weekly and quarterly Metrics Scorecard *results* match what you have *targeted*. We will refer to these tasks as *Fixed Daily Activities* or FDAs.

Some FDAs need to be done each day, while others are performed weekly, monthly, or quarterly (such as reports). The key point to keep is mind is that these are critical tasks. Even though there will be a different set of tasks from day-to-day, each set must be performed faithfully on a daily basis. To tie them closely to your quarterly and weekly Metrics Scorecards, we suggest breaking your FDA list into five separate categories:

- **Client Retention FDAs** – Focused specifically on retaining current clients who match your *Ideal Client Profile*.

- **Client Upgrade FDAs** – Focused specifically on upgrading existing clients you believe can be upgraded to the Ideal Client level within the next year (or so).

- **Client Attracting FDAs** – Focused specifically on attracting new clients who match your *Ideal Client Profile*.

- **Operational FDAs** – Focused on all the paperwork including daily, weekly, monthly, quarterly, and yearly reporting and administrative tasks related to attracting, servicing, and retaining clients. The creation and maintenance of yearly, quarterly, and weekly Metrics Scorecards should be included in this list of FDAs.

- **Administrative FDAs** – Focused on supporting other areas of non-client related responsibility, plus keeping current with inner-company requirements.

Each Team Member should be asked to develop individual sets of lists. Then meet as a Team to consolidate those lists and assign specific FDAs to specific Team Members. Make certain everyone has transferred assigned FDAs to their daily planner. If you share an electronic daily planner system, you have two advantages. First, you can make certain every FDA has been transferred to the system. Second, everyone can see how the Team functions at the most basic interrelated task level.

You'll be encouraged to know that our "Thanksgiving" Wealth Management Team did get back on track, thanks to their Metrics Scorecards, and are now enjoying tremendous growth. But equally important, they made the paradigm shift in how they keep score.

Beware of External Impact Factors

Allow me to share another wirehouse story to illustrate how easy it is to become pulled back to the old paradigm.

While helping a group of top producers to develop Wealth Management Teams based on our 21st Century Financial Practice™ *model, despite the natural challenge of breaking behavioral and attitudinal habit patterns all seemed to be going well. A lot of hard work with follow-up conference calls, homework assignments, and meetings were required; but exciting progress was being made. And then it happened!*

*The firm's National Sales Department unveiled a "**New Account Opening Campaign**" for the third quarter. Desperate to inject fuel into their distribution force after a slow summer, they distributed a brochure announcing all the reward levels: Palm Pilots, cellular phones, trips, etc., and a corresponding PowerPoint® presentation that every branch manager was required to use during their first sales meeting in September.*

You know exactly what happened. The fear of "slipping production" is difficult for any organization to ignore and short-term incentives have always effectively created spurts of activity. Therefore, why not use a proven tactic to get things rolling again?

The problem comes in defining the "things." In the midst of a paradigm shift it would be easy, under pressure, to revert back instead of courageously moving forward. Pressured by sagging production, not everyone will be supportive. That's why you must be very protective of your new *21st Century Metrics System*. In the case mentioned above, it simply took a conference call with all the Wealth Management Teams I was working with in the firm to help them keep focused on their scorecards and FDAs.

It's important to recognize that the creation of your Metrics Scorecards and assignment of Fixed Daily Activities (FDAs) to Team Members firmly establishes your *21st Century Metrics System*. So embrace them! Use them! This system will breathe life into your 5-Year Business Plan, facilitate your paradigm shift, and provide you with many opportunities to celebrate your success along the way. Soon you will be looking back and waving "goodbye" to your competitors.

Attracting, Qualifying and Closing Affluent Prospects

It is not enough to have a good mind.
The main thing is to use it well.

Descartes

Y ou have already heard the good news; affluent Americans are searching for unbiased financial advice and they want solutions for the multidimensional aspects of their personal finances. But do you understand the role word-of-mouth influence is going to play in attracting, qualifying and closing prospects that fit your *Ideal Client Profile?*

These highly coveted consumers make the majority of their decisions, especially when it involves one of four key dimensions of life, by talking and discussing various aspects of those dimensions with people they respect. Your good fortune is that one of those dimensions is your world, *financial health* (the other three are *personal health, family health,* and *spiritual health*). That's why a Financial Advisor's acquisition cost of attracting Affluent Investors has been considered to be zero. You probably experienced this in your old sales practice, where many of your best clients came by word-of-mouth (or referral).

In the May 2001 edition of *American Demographics*, Rebecca Gardyn reports that a survey by HNW Digital revealed that 86% of Americans with household incomes of $150,000 or more and asset values of $500,000 or more (not including primary residence) rank financial success and secu-

---

rity as being important to their overall happiness. The conclusion is that "The opportunity is there for the financial service and banking industries to really deepen their relationships … to help them maintain this happiness." It seems the more we know about Affluent Investors, the better it gets. Here's an example of how one man capitalized on his opportunity.

Bob is a 45-year old Financial Advisor with six years of experience (an attorney in another life), leading a vertical Wealth Management Team with two Specialists. A retired physician with a tax problem was referred to Bob by one of his clients. Although this Affluent Investor already had two other Financial Advisors who both had substantial accounts, word-of-mouth influence landed him, tax problem in hand, in Bob's office.

Three months later, tax problem solved, the new client who was not yet ideal but possessed strong potential, called Bob and asked for a proposal. The physician client wanted to consolidate his three accounts with one group. Bob went right to work, hoping that solving the tax problem would at least give him a chance in the competition with the other two Advisors. The next morning Bob received another call from the physician who said, "I hope you haven't spent much time working on that proposal, Bob. I've already made up my mind, and am moving all of my assets to you. Also, I have a friend who is interested in working with you, if you have the time."

Consider the outcome! Bob closed a $7.5 million relationship and was introduced to a $5 million ideal prospect. No cold calling, mass mailing campaign, free seminar or any other traditional marketing tactic can produce those results. In this case, the acquisition cost was "zero." It came to Bob *through word-of-mouth influence. However, no one can just sit around waiting for referrals to come his or her way. Word-of-mouth influence must become a proactive process.*

"Find a need and fill it" is about the shortest, to-the-point definition of marketing that I recall ever hearing. It suggests that the essence of marketing centers around two basic concepts: *find* and *fill*. Let's look at each.

We certainly did *find a need* when we conducted our research. In Chapter 1, we defined an Affluent Investor market of 16.3 million households with a net worth of between $500,000 and $5 million; and what they need is help with managing their wealth. You remember too that we also quoted conversations with established Financial Advisors indicating that they "have more clients than they can handle," "wish they weren't so busy" and have "raised their minimums to better manage the flow of new clients." The need has been found, but are you ready to *fill it*? If you still depend entirely on traditional sales and marketing tactics, you are not ready.

Why do I say that? Well, first of all, the new clients you seek are very concerned with *protecting* the wealth they already have. For many, that is their most important concern. As their wealth becomes public knowledge, more people will try to sell them something. Consequently, traditional marketing techniques and sales pitches turn them off. They naturally resist any type of broad, impersonal marketing approach, as well as the person using the approach; and that includes direct mailings, e-mail marketing, cold calls, seminar invitations and other variations on that theme.

Secondly, people in the marketing segments that you wish to target are looking for a competent unbiased Financial Advisor who can help them with a wide range of financial protection, investment and disbursement needs – all the way from budgeting to estate planning and a half dozen other services in-between. Marketing experts will tell you that mailings, cold calls, and seminar invitations need to be narrowly focused on a specific financial need in order to have any chance of success. But if you follow that advice, you risk coming across as a one-dimensional financial salesperson rather than the multidimensional financial solutions provider the affluent seek.

Third, no Affluent Investor is going to accept the advice and guidance of someone they are not absolutely certain they can *trust* when the protection, investment and disbursement of that much wealth is involved. In this case, *trust* is a huge concept. They need to trust your competence and your integrity. So, they often won't even let you approach them if you are not introduced or referred by an individual they already like and trust.

Assuming you have the integrity, not an assumption to be taken lightly in the real world, your challenge in marketing to the affluent is to build your *21st Century Financial Practice™*. As fundamental as this might appear, many financial professionals who are already steeped in the sales and marketing mode, skip all the necessary retooling we've discussed up to this point and focus on marketing. That is a big mistake! Affluent Investors (your Ideal Clients) are not stupid; and purchasing a brochure, mastering a few sophisticated phrases or posturing as something that you are not, will not work. Even if someone is fooled into doing business with this approach, they'll soon discover that they have been duped and will leave spreading *negative* word-of-mouth influence.

Remember the three largest performance expectations gaps Affluent Investors reported during our research: not receiving satisfactory *value* for the fees paid, not trusting the *quality* of the advice received, and not trusting that the advice received is *always* in their best interest. Those results are the product of transaction-based, product pushing, sales and marketing tactics that have been prevalent throughout the financial services industry, until now!

Focusing Your Client Development Efforts

To successfully achieve your 5-Year Business Plan, your Wealth Management Team must initiate two parallel tracks of client development: *internal* and *external*.

- **Internal Client Development** involves your efforts to *retain* current clients who match your *Ideal Client Profile* as well as efforts to *upgrade* clients you believe can match your *Ideal Client Profile* during the next 12 to 18 months. This requires building your *Financial Advisory* and *Operational Efficiency Processes* to deliver your value agenda.

- **External Client Development** involves your efforts to *add* to your Ideal Client base through the process of attracting, qualifying, and closing affluent prospects. You will be using the same processes developed for your Internal Client Development since you will be delivering the same value agenda.

Internal Client Development

Retaining and *upgrading* desirable clients will only happen if you have done the work presented back in Chapter 4 and have an *Ideal Client Profile* in place which provides specific criteria that your Team is using to define what is "desirable" about the clients you seek. In addition, your Team must perform the Fixed Daily Activities (FDAs) that you identified in Chapter 5; particularly the *Client Retention* and *Client Upgrade* FDAs. All Team Members must judiciously monitor retaining and upgrading activity, using the *Weekly Metrics Scorecard* that you initiated in Chapter 5, in order to make certain that activities are completed on a timely basis.

You may be anxious to move on to the External Client Development track, and that's understandable. "More clients" has been the battle cry of the sales and marketing model, and it's hard to push that paradigm aside. However, if you are not effectively building an Ideal Client base by retaining and upgrading current clients, you will fail to build the network and develop the expertise you need to effectively attract new Affluent Investors. You will then run the risk of reverting back to the old sales and marketing tactics that Affluent Investors resist.

Keep in mind that your existing clients, who are marked for upgrading to Ideal Clients, already know you. Hopefully they trust you and have a good working professional relationship with you. By building your *processes*, repositioning yourself as a multidimensional solutions provider who is process driven, you will gain the requisite confidence for attracting, qualifying, closing, and servicing new Ideal Clients.

However, beware! Internal Business Development is uncomfortable as you reinvent yourself right in front of your clients. There may be a tendency to skip over this step by various forms of rationalization such as, "I already have all their money," "They already view me as multidimensional," or "I'll get to it later." But, don't buy into this subconscious chatter because there is gold within your existing client base, if mined properly.

Nobody could have convinced Barry that he would uncover $250 million in assets during the first three weeks of meeting with existing clients and beginning his repositioning process. Actually, three clients contributed $150 million to the figure and another nine clients contributed the other $100 million. Regardless of how the figures broke down, the reality was that each of these clients was capable of being upgraded to meet Barry's Ideal Client Profile *of three mil-*

lion investable dollars; and not one of the 12 had more than $750,000 with him at the time.

Blinded by his enthusiasm, Barry assured me he was going to get all $250 million because these people trusted him and he had developed an excellent relationship with them over the years. Well, when he arrived back "on earth" about four months later, he had brought in $35 million in new assets from his Internal Business Development campaign – and wasn't complaining. The confidence he gained through this type of repositioning success was perfect fuel for his External Business Development; and he was still working on the remaining $215 million!

External Client Development

This is the track that you are probably eager to master. If the old sales and marketing tactics don't work with Affluent Investors, there must be a better way. So, what is that "better way"? How do you start? What will it take to become expert at it?

Hopefully you will already have experienced Internal Business Development successes to bolster your confidence. The lesson to be learned from Barry's experience is that being engaged in the process boosts your confidence, possibly as much as seeing the amount of asset gain achieved in the effort.

The External Client Development track can be broken down into three major processes.

- **Attracting** the Affluent Investor prospects you desire.

- **Qualifying** those prospects that are potential Ideal Clients.

- **Closing** potential Ideal Clients.

Attracting Affluent Investor Prospects

Your Wealth Management Team needs a marketing strategy that will attract Affluent Investor prospects like a magnet. We have emphasized over and over that mailings, cold calls, seminars and the like are not the ticket to get you in their door. As you have read and done your homework, you have created the magnetic appeal you need. Now you simply need to spread it, which involves the process of *networking*.

Networking bypasses the three reasons traditional tactics don't work. It builds on the trust relationships that people you know have established with people that they know. In order to effectively tap into Affluent Investor networks you must *target* the right prospects and *connect* with the prospects you target. We'll look at each in some detail.

1. **Target the right prospects**. When you developed your *Ideal Client Profile*, you selected up to three market segments as your focus (Chapter 4). The place to begin attracting prospects who match that profile is to target a specific niche within one of the segments you selected.

   Select a segment from your *Ideal Client Profile*, one in which key individuals on your Team can tap the following to help you zero in on a specific niche within that segment.

   - Your collective circles of influence such as clients, friends and family.

   - Your professional backgrounds and the collective knowledge you have gained from them.

   - Your areas of financial specialty that might address specific needs.

Example: You identify best with those who have achieved their own wealth, so you focus on the Generators of Wealth target market. The segment within that market that best matches the above three criteria is Self-Employed Medical Professionals, since you already have three doctors as clients, a wife who was a nurse and a niece in medical school. The solutions you offer should match this niche well.

That's a great start, but the more focused you are the better, so another important criterion to consider is:

- Do you have a client or know someone influential who will help you open doors?

Example: One of your wealthiest clients, one with whom you have great rapport, is an orthopedic surgeon. You go to an Internet search engine and enter "orthopedic surgery" and discover the New England Orthopedic Surgeons web site (right in your backyard!). There's even a physician and clinical staff director. That information, along with your client as a potential *Internal Advocate*, convinces you to focus on this niche.

Next, it's important to find ways to connect with the Affluent Investor prospects within your targeted niche.

2. **Connect with targeted prospects**. First of all, you need to learn everything you can about your targeted niche. "Everything" may be stretching things a bit, but it's very important that you understand the challenges that people in your targeted niche face in order to make wise decisions about how they allocate their financial resources. Knowing everything you can means learning about those challenges and under-

standing how they attempt to meet them. As you learn about their world, you will also begin to discover interesting possibilities for networking select Team Members into their path. The following diagram helps to illustrate the interactions.

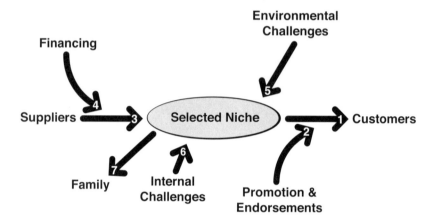

- **Customers (1)** – Unless they are Receivers of Wealth, your prospects need customers/clients/patients in order to continue accumulating wealth. Your current clients, friends, family, etc. could become or might know others who could become customers of an individual you wish to attract.

- **Promotion and Endorsements (2)** – To attract customers/ clients/patients, your prospects need to promote their business. As you become expert at soliciting referrals and building alliances, you can help them develop theirs. Endorsements of them by Team Members could also open doors for your prospects.

- **Suppliers (3)** – Whether they are in business or not, your prospects purchase products and services. Hopefully, you will become one of their suppliers. Helping them find reliable suppliers for other key purchases could help make that happen. By putting two prospects together, you help one find a supplier and the other a customer.

- **Financing (4)** – Despite their wealth, your prospects don't pay cash for everything, especially when it comes to financing the expansion of their business. Money is your area of expertise, but often not theirs. Think of the possibilities in helping people find good money sources and helping them negotiate loans at a good rate.

- **Environmental Challenges (5)** – There are governmental regulations, competitors, and a variety of other challenges outside their organization over which people often feel they have little, if any, control. When specific Team Members join prospective clients in their causes, you show them that you have their best interests at heart.

- **Internal Challenges (6)** – Within their business and the other organizations with whom they affiliate, many prospects face internal organizational challenges about which specific Team Members may have some expertise – even beyond financial matters. Or you may know people you can network into those situations.

- **Family (7)** – Many prospects have family considerations that you can help them address, and there may be family members who also need your services.

The principle at work here is: *give now – receive later*. The purpose of these efforts is to build a level of trust that leads them to say, "Now, about my finances…"

At this point, you are probably thinking that trying to do all those things for all those people is unrealistic, and you're right. What you need to do is *focus* and there are three ways you do that.

- As you learn more and more about the world of your selected niche, focus in on two or three of the seven networking areas in which your Wealth Management Team can serve them best. Base that decision on *what* you have learned about their most immediate needs, *what* you know that you can do as a Team, and *who* you know that you can rely on for help.

- As you discover the places where they "hang out," focus your networking efforts on finding *Internal Advocates*. Internal Advocates are those people who also "hang out" there and are willing to help you get in and meet the people you have targeted. Begin by looking for Internal Advocates among your clients (see the *Example* cited earlier).

- There are two ways that select Team Members can use an *Internal Advocate* to help target individuals within your selected niche. First, target individuals you want to meet and ask your Internal Advocate for an introduction or referral. Do your homework so you know exactly why you want to meet that individual and know as much about them as you can. Second, ask your Internal Advocates to identify people in your niche that they believe would benefit from knowing you. Again, you want to learn as much as you can about these people as well.

Referrals are a great tactic for attracting new clients, but the real purpose of networking is to get something even better – introductions. That's where you start, asking Internal Advocates to invite you to events and activities where they can introduce you to individuals (the type of individuals you have targeted). Your hope is that the resulting conversation will lead to an appointment with that individual; and that is a real possibility if you listen for the right clues. Either way, you are stimulating word-of-mouth influence and your magnetism.

Your best opportunity to convince any prospect of your value to them occurs when they reveal what we call an *Impact Point* relating to their financial well-being. Your Internal Advocate should introduce you as a Financial Advisor and add whatever accolades they choose. Then, through listening and questioning, you will hear people commenting about:

- Having a financial opportunity/problem they don't know how to address.
- Looking for someone to help them manage their finances and/or investments.
- Being dissatisfied with their current broker, insurance agent, advisor, etc.
- Being discouraged by stock market fluctuations.
- Selling their business or practice.
- Getting ready to retire.
- Making a public stock offering.
- Engaging in a business merger.
- Selling a capital asset.
- Funding their qualified retirement plan.
- Exercising stock options.
- Being promoted or moving to a new job at higher income, bonuses, etc.
- Receiving a large bonus or commission check.
- Having a CD mature.
- Being frustrated because CD rates drop.
- Having bonds called.
- Receiving IRA rollover assets.

- Receiving an inheritance.
- Facing divorce.
- Grieving the death of a parent, spouse, or other close family member.

Connecting with Affluent Investor prospects requires that you be alert enough to identify any Impact Points – and then be able to articulate a clear *value proposition* in order to capitalize on the door just opened to you.

As you go through the above checklist and determine those Impact Points for which you can provide expert solutions, prepare yourself for those opportunities by preparing a *value proposition* statement you can use for each. For example, if you discover that someone is about to retire, you might say:

> *I have considerable experience helping retired clients make smart choices about their investments. I take great care to help clients evaluate options and select the ones that are best for them.*

That's as far as you should go when responding to an Impact Point – except to suggest a later appointment if they would be interested in learning more. Since you were introduced to them by someone they trust; and you have responded to a need that they mentioned, you have significantly increased the probability of a positive response and an opportunity to build trust in your own right. When you meet for that appointment, your first task will be to qualify them as an Ideal Client prospect.

Qualifying Ideal Client Prospects

When you are able to use an Impact Point as the basis for scheduling an appointment with an affluent prospect, you know at least one reason why they could use your services. That's a great beginning, but that does not necessarily qualify them as a prospective Ideal Client.

You *qualify* someone so that neither of you will waste time pursuing a professional relationship that just isn't going to happen. You're already well into the qualifying process if you:

- Are pursuing people in a well-defined market niche.

- Are introduced to, referred to, or in some other way net-worked to an individual by someone who knows your Ideal Client Profile minimum investable assets requirement.

This last item suggests the necessity to inform your Internal Advocates of the minimum investable asset requirement you established when developing your *Ideal Client Profile*. Armed with that important piece of information, they may introduce or refer you to fewer people – but they will be the right people in terms of your wealth criteria.

There are three steps in the qualifying process:

1. **Ask key questions** that will help clarify their needs and the type of relationship you can expect to have with them.

   Begin the appointment by asking a series of questions to better understand the prospect – and to let them know that you want to understand. Here are some excellent questions for that purpose; and be prepared to take notes.

   - *Could you tell me something about your background?*

     This should reveal family background and help identify key values that will likely influence their investment decisions.

   - *Could you tell me about your work and how you achieved your present success?*

This should reveal their philosophy and approach to building wealth and help you gain an initial assessment of their attitudes toward risk.

- *Are there any key financial challenges you presently face?*

  This should confirm the initial Impact Point you identified plus reveal other areas where they need and desire help. This is a key question for qualifying them as a potential client.

- *Are there people other than yourself whose future is or will be impacted by those financial challenges?*

  This should help clarify important family and professional connections that will impact financial decisions. You might want to use follow-up questions to learn more about some of those relationships.

- *What would you want from someone who serves you in a Financial Advisory capacity?*

  This should help clarify the type of advisor-client relationship that would emerge if they became your client. It will probably take a series of questions for you to do that. Here are some things you want to discover.

  - Some love to play the market and will want to make all the decisions. They will mostly want information from you. They will also tend to keep working with multiple brokers and consequently may not meet all your *Ideal Client Profile* criteria.

  - Others will see managing their money as a burden. They will want the total solution from you, and they will be delighted to discover they can trust you, and only you, to advise them. They will also tend to be conservative investors. Assuming they meet all your *Ideal Client Profile* criteria, these make great clients.

- In between are those who have a real interest in managing money and are fascinated with the various financial products. They will want you to help them achieve wealth, but with minimum risk. Gaining their trust is a real challenge, and they tend to keep switching advisors over time.

2. **Explain who you are**, what you do, and how they will benefit from working with you. Once you have a feel for the type of relationship they envision, it's a good time to:

- Introduce your Wealth Management Team Members.

- Review your *Financial Advisory Process* (covered in Chapter 8).

Use your promotional piece to walk them through this information, and then leave the piece with them for future reference.

3. **Ask the BIG question**.

If their answers suggest a good match, complete the qualification process by making certain that they can meet your *Ideal Client Profile* investable assets minimum. If they do, your next step will be to get your potential client to commit to working with you.

Closing Potential Ideal Clients

At this point, you will be ready to close – which involves the prospective client making a commitment to work with you. A simple approach to use when you have reached that point goes like this:

- **Based on** … (a summary of what *they said* when answering your questions plus *their response* to what you presented).

- **I would like to suggest that** … (the specific action you would like them to take and a time line, which could be any of the following).
    - we proceed with the first step described in our promotional piece.
    - we prepare a Letter of Agreement for you to review and sign.
    - we make an appointment to meet on (date) _____ and begin the next step.

- **Would that be** … (use your own style here).
    - agreeable to you?
    - a good next step for your?
    - the best way for us to proceed from here?

This approach is simple to learn, and it leaves no doubt about *what* you are suggesting, *why* you are suggesting it, and *when* it is to be completed. Their response to the "Would that be …" ending will tell you exactly where they are at this point.

If they are not ready to take your suggested action, you can follow up with questions like:

- "Is there a problem with what I have suggested?"

- "Are there some other issues that need to be resolved first?"

- "Would you mind telling me what is causing you to hesitate at this time?"

- "Have I offended you in any way with what I have suggested?"

This is a business relationship you're trying to establish, not a social one. Do not hesitate to ask why they are not ready to establish that relationship. In most cases, they will appreciate your desire to understand why the connection has not been made.

Internal and External Client Development are two tracks that must be traveled together to avoid a derailment of your business. You know what to do and you have the tools to help you. All you need is the courage to step out and do it.

Every member of your Wealth Management Team will need to understand that their level of professionalism represents the perceived value of the product being offered to your affluent clientele and prospects. Everything matters, from the way your phones are answered to the image you present. Everything and everybody counts.

In Chapters 7 and 8, you'll learn how to advise all those retained, upgraded, and new Ideal Clients.

The
Financial Advisory
Process

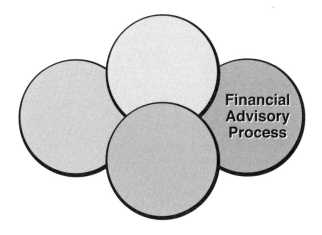

Chapter 7
Meeting the Multi-Dimensional Financial Needs
Of Affluent Clients

Chapter 8
Designing an Effective Financial Advisory Process

Meeting the Multi-Dimensional Financial Needs of Affluent Clients

---

There are always opportunities
through which businessmen (women)
can profit handsomely if they
will only recognize and seize them...

J. Paul Getty

The rules of engagement are clear. The Affluent Investors you seek to attract are better informed. They will have at least some working knowledge of the multiple asset management options available to them. They have higher expectations. They tend to be somewhat cynical toward the world of financial services. And because of their multi-dimensional financial needs, many are choosing to manage their assets through a combination of channels:

- Self-managing some assets by using on-line services and information.

- Utilizing the services of a money manager for major investments.

- Seeking the guidance of various Financial Advisors for other areas.

It's the motive behind those choices that is so important. It goes right back to the three most critical performance gaps uncovered in our research.

The issue is *trust*. Knowing they have options, Affluent Investors will seek guidance and advice from those sources that they believe will:

- Provide satisfactory value for fees and commissions paid.

- Give advice that is always in their best interest.

- Provide high-quality and trustworthy information for making financial and investment decisions.

In the last chapter, you learned about the strategies, tactics, and skills needed for both Internal and External Client Development. You know what it takes to retain and upgrade current clients to Ideal Client status. You know what's required to attract, qualify, and close new Affluent Investors who match your *Ideal Client Profile*. The question now is, "Once you've got 'em, what're you gonna give 'em?" In other words:

What are you prepared to do to meet the multidimensional financial needs of affluent clients and, in the process, gain their trust?

The good news is that many Affluent Investors want one source – a trusted Wealth Management Team (like yours!) who can advise them in all the multidimensional aspects of their personal finances. Why? Because it brings a degree of simplicity to their time crunched, complex, affluent lives within the complex world of financial services.

To become that designated Team, you will need to offer highly competent, integrated *solutions* in 8 Key Financial Advisory Categories. That does not mean that your key Team Members must become experts in every area, although you must be able to talk intelligently about each; but your individual expertise will reside in two or possibly three areas. In addition, you will need to develop strong professional arrangements with others who can competently fill in the other pieces of the Financial Advisory puzzle.

Evaluating Your Present
Wealth Management Team Performance

Following are brief descriptions of the 8 Key Financial Advisory Categories that are the focus of building a successful *21st Century Financial Practice™*. Not every category will apply to every client, and the specific application of each category will differ from client to client. Collectively, however, you can expect all categories to play a role in your success.

As you read through the descriptions, consider the following:

- Do you offer anything in that category? You may want to place a check mark in front of those that you can answer with *yes*.

- *If yes* – which of the specific solutions and services do you presently offer to clients? Again, you may want to place a check mark in front of those you do offer.

1. Budgeting, Cash Flow Management, and Determining Net Worth

Budgeting focuses on helping your client to control spending. It includes:

- Having clients pull together and set up a system for maintaining a detailed and accurate account of income and spending.

- Helping clients budget spending.

- Guiding clients if they are burdened with excessive debt, especially if they have difficulty with controlling spending.

- Guiding clients in creating and committing to a current year expense budget.

- Helping clients project future income and expenses and create projected budgets to reflect anticipated changes.

Cash Flow Management focuses on defining cash inputs, establishing and maintaining a reserve of cash and near cash equivalents, and the systematic maintenance of cash surplus for investment purposes. It includes:

- Helping clients explore debt consolidation and restructure to pay off all credit card and other short-term debt to improve cash flow.

- Helping clients explore investment reallocation to improve cash flow.

- Guiding clients in creating and committing to a cash flow budget for the current year.

- Helping clients project what impact future projected budgets will have on cash flow and create projected cash flow budgets to reflect those changes.

Determining Net Worth focuses on defining current assets and liabilities and constructing a *Net Worth Statement*. It includes:

- Helping clients construct a current *Net Worth Statement*. Assets are categorized as liquid, personal, and investment. Liabilities are classified as short-term and long-term.

- Using the current statement as a basis for helping clients determine an appropriate net worth planning strategy that deals with goal setting and debt reduction plus seeking higher investment return to meet those goals.

2. **Insurance Planning**

Insurance focuses on helping clients provide for risks that can cause serious financial loss – to pay medical bills, to replace or repair such tangible items as homes and vehicles, to replace income lost to disability, or to maintain a standard of living after the death of a spouse or other loved one. Insurance is divided into two categories:

Life and Health, which includes:

- Term life, whole life, universal life, variable life.

- Health insurance.

- Disability insurance.

- Long-term care.

Property and Casualty, which includes:

- Home owners insurance.

- Automobile and other vehicle insurance.

- Liability insurance.

3. **Investment Administration (Asset Management)**

The focus is on helping clients determine the amount available for investing, decide how that amount is to be invested, and calculate how the investment income will contribute to the cash flow budgets.

This requires *skillful analysis of the following investment criteria*:

- Your client's risk tolerance level.

- Your client's time frame for achieving each financial objective.

- Liquidity needs along with the ease with which each investment can be bought and sold – plus the ability to convert investments into cash without losing a significant part of the principle.

- Income tax considerations – including your client's tax bracket and available tax credits.

- The importance of diversification to spread the risk among different asset classes and investment instruments.

- Who should act as the client's broker-dealer?

- Their desire to participate in on-line investing, if any.

4. **Education Planning**

Education Planning focuses on identifying current and future costs of education, projecting personal education goals plus those for their children, and determining the financial needs by year through to the end of those educational activities. This will include helping clients to:

- Create an educational budget.

- Complete a trial financial aid test.

- Find sources where they and their children can learn about educational options.

- Plan college financial aid strategies while their children are still in high school.

- Evaluate each financial aid award and then make strategy adjustments accordingly.

5. **Tax Planning**

Tax Planning involves helping clients find potential tax savings through reducing or shifting current or future income tax liabilities. This includes:

- Guiding clients in deferring income and/or accelerating expenses at year-end.

- Helping clients choose strategies to realize losses or gains through a wide range of allowable actions.

6. **Retirement Planning**

Retirement Planning focuses on determining the amount needed/ desired upon retirement and then determining which retirement plan options will best meet those goals. This includes:

- Helping clients plan how they will accumulate money using qualified, personal, and/or nonqualified plans.

- Helping clients maximize assets during their working years.

- Determining with clients the best methods and timing for withdrawing retirement income.

7. **Estate Planning**

Estate Planning involves identifying beneficiaries and what they are to receive both during life and upon death. This includes:

- Making certain you and your clients know about available estate planning techniques and tools.

- Making certain that those techniques and tools are used skill-fully to achieve the client's estate plan goals.

- Helping clients determine how they will transfer property during their life through gifts in order to reduce the size of the potential probate estate while also avoiding a tax burden on beneficiaries.

- Helping clients determine how property will be transferred at death by means of a will, intestate, contract, trust, and/or operation of law.

8. **Charitable Giving**

Focuses on understanding the values and desires of your clients and their families. Helps them enhance their quality of life through a sensible Charitable Giving Plan. This includes:

- Getting to know your clients and their families well enough to understand the values and desires that drive them.

- Helping clients identify charitable giving opportunities that fit within their value structure while helping to minimize their tax liability.

- Having clients develop a Charitable Giving Plan to be incorporated into their Cash Flow and Expense Budgets.

With the above inventory, you're ready to evaluate your *present performance* and *competency* in each of the 8 Key Financial Advisory Categories.

A. **Performance** – The first question is: Do you offer this category (yes or no)? If you have already checked the above categories and specific services you offer, you know the answer to that question.

Offering is one thing; being paid for it is another. The next question is what percent of your clients are paying you for the services you checked? Begin with your *Top 25 Net Profit Contribution Clients*, especially those who match your *Ideal Client Profile* (see Chapter 4). Your goal will be to do the following:

- Identify exactly which of the 8 Key Financial Advisory Categories you are providing for each existing Ideal Client you will be working to retain, as well as each existing client you expect to upgrade to the Ideal Client level within the next 12 to 18 months. This is the service foundation from which you will build your *21st Century Financial Practice™*.

- Look at that same group of clients you wish to retain and upgrade, and explore as a Team, other categories you all believe they might want right now – or could be persuaded to accept if you were able to offer these categories at the highest level of competence.

B. **Competency** – The second question is: How much knowledge and skill does your Wealth Management Team collectively possess in each category? In this case, knowledge and skill have specific meanings.

- *Knowledge* is knowing what is involved in providing competent advice and where to find current information to meet all needs for all situations.

- *Skill* is your ability to apply your knowledge through competently utilizing the following six Financial Advisory tasks:

  - *Profile* – collect the right information from the individual and organize it in such a way that it defines and displays important interrelationships relating to that category.

  - *Educate* – present and clearly explain financial information in terms the individual understands, including how it links to all aspects of their financial picture

  - *Analyze* – define important cause-effect relationships relating to short-term and long-term financial decisions, to

explain those relationships in terms the individual understands, and to help the individual understand the short-
term and long-term choices available.

- *Solve* – incorporate the individual's values, interests,
  dreams, etc. into the decision-making process and help
  the individual use that input to narrow down and make a
  final choice.

- *Implement* – help the individual put their choices into
  action in a timely and efficient manner.

- *Monitor* – establish an appropriate checkup method and
  schedule that is both acceptable to and motivating for
  your client.

The following chart will help you summarize your present performance and competency for each of the 8 Key Financial Advisory Categories. Instructions for completion are noted below.

Category	Offer (yes/no)	% Clients Use	Competency
Budgeting, Cash flow, Net Worth			
Insurance Planning			
Investment Administration			
Education Planning			
Tax Planning			
Retirement Planning			
Estate Planning			
Charitable Giving			

- *Offer (yes/no)* column – Write "Yes" in those categories you
  currently offer.

- *% Clients Use* column – First determine whether you are going to calculate the percentage of:

  a) All present clients,

  b) Your *Top 25 Net Profile Contribution Clients*, or

  c) Those clients you have targeted to retain and upgrade.

  When you calculate, remember that you want the percentage of those *who presently use you for this service.* If some pay you directly for that service and others don't, you may also want to separate the "don't pay" group from the others.

- *Competency* column – use the scale below to indicate your Wealth Management Team's collective level of knowledge and skill in each category.

High knowledge and skill	–	5
High knowledge, moderate skill	–	4
Moderate knowledge and skill	–	3
Moderate knowledge, low skill	–	2
Low knowledge and skill	–	1
No knowledge or skill	–	0

Your Financial Advisory Development Plan

Here is where you must be careful not to assume; it can lead to arrogance. The following is a case in point.

> *I had just completed a program for a group of Independent Financial Planners; some worked out of their homes, some in key-man offices and others in a collective grouping*

within shared office space. Most were from the insurance world, and all were targeting the affluent.

The professionalism and sophistication of this group was impressive. They were accustomed to both the long lead times required when romancing larger clients and to providing multiple insurance solutions. Most needed to learn more about investments, and most had far too many clients. But all were eager to learn, grow, and make whatever changes necessary.

Two days later I was conducting a similar workshop for a group of council level brokers. Like the Independent Financial Planners, this group was professional, sophisticated, and good at what they did – investments. They were basically a group of successful one-dimensional stockbrokers. The biggest difference was their arrogance.

When I mentioned having recently worked with the group of Independent Financial Planners, they responded with snickers, jokes, and disparaging remarks that were not only based on false assumptions, but also provided tremendous insight into their own insecurities. You can be sure that they left that meeting with a newfound respect for this emerging competitor. I pointed out that if they truly wanted to become multidimensional solutions providers, there probably was more they needed to learn than the group of Independent Financial Planners.

Adding services and expanding knowledge and skill does not just happen. It requires planned, intentional effort. Arrogance and assumptions have no place in the process. At the beginning of this chapter we asked, "What are you prepared to do to meet the multidimensional financial needs of Affluent Investor clients and, in the process, gain their trust?"

They don't care whether their go-to Wealth Management Team evolved from an insurance, stockbroker, accounting, or legal background. They are concerned about your Team's ability to deliver the goods.

But you need not worry, because you have already taken the first step by going through the above list of services and the results told you two important things. You know what you offer, what you know, and what you can do. You also know what you don't offer, what you don't know, and what you are not yet able to do. That is incredibly valuable information.

If you have *walked our talk* from Chapter 1 on, you are now miles ahead of your competition. You know which clients you want to attract and have a marketing strategy and tactics in place. You have also identified the gap that exists between where you are and where you need to be in terms of the solutions and services you offer. That's a great place to be, because you can now draw up a development plan to close that gap and here's how to do it.

1. Financial planning certification is an important step toward closing the gap. Most important is the *Certified Financial Planner (CFP)* designation. As of August 31, 2001, there were 37,796 CFP licensees In the United States – with more than 1,400 having been added since the beginning of that year.

   The CFP requirements include an education program that covers a wide spectrum of financial planning categories. This makes it especially valuable for individuals wanting to expand their expertise, whether they come from a CPA, investment, insurance, or other background. If key members of your Wealth Management Team have not yet made this step, explore the following web site.

   CFP Board of Standards – *http://www.cfp-board.org/*

Other Financial Advisor certifications you can consider include: PFS, CFA, ChFC, RIA, CIMA, and CLU. Now that Merrill Lynch is putting its money where their young Financial Advisors' certifications are, many other firms will follow. In year five of their tenure, all Merrill trainees can earn a $100,000 bonus if they have earned a CFP, CFA, ChFC, or CIMA designation. Within the first year, all their trainees must obtain Merrill's internal financial planning designation, Certified Financial Manager. The times certainly are changing!

2. Each individual on your Wealth Management Team who will be directly involved in the *Financial Advisory Process* (see Chapter 8) needs to determine which area or areas (three maximum) will become their specialty. That means achieving a competency level of 5 – a high level of knowledge and skill in all aspects of that category.

3. When your Wealth Management Team has collectively determined who will specialize in what, inventory the specific areas that will be covered by Team Members. Then determine how you will arrange to cover each of the categories not already included. You have several options.

- *Hire* – This individual will become your employee.

- *Contract* – You will contract to use their services on a fee basis, as needed.

- *Partner* – You will establish a mutual exchange of knowledge and services, operating on a fee and/or profit sharing basis.

- *Other* – You may be aware of individuals and have a unique type of relationship in mind, or have already established one with them.

4. Each Team Member, who has any contact with clients, needs to become conversant with *all* of the Financial Advisory categories you will be offering. Being conversant involves several important capabilities.

- Knowing all the types of solutions and services offered in each category.

- Being familiar with the various instruments used and the basic terminology relating to each category.

- Knowing what they don't know – and who to bring into the conversation when they are placed into an "I don't know" situation.

The best source for cross training is each other. Since those who advise need to learn how to "teach" clients in terms that they will understand, have Team Members "practice" on each other. The more you teach each other, the more effective you will become when advising clients.

Other sources for expanding your working knowledge within the various Financial Advisory categories are the Specialists with whom you have developed a strategic alliance. Nobody does this any better than Amy.

Amy is a Financial Advisor in Los Angeles and former class-action attorney (albeit a junior attorney) in a major firm. Her objective in becoming a Financial Advisor is two-fold: to provide legitimate financial solutions to people who have acquired sudden windfalls of wealth and to be compensated for it. She feels that her former law firm took advantage of her as a junior attorney.

Being aware of what is needed to properly serve these people endowed with sudden wealth, Amy created the model of being a multidimensional solutions provider long before leaving her law firm. Upon striking out on her own as an independent, she immediately created a strategic alliance with two estate-planning attorneys and two tax specialists.

When a client or prospect needs estate work or sophisticated tax advice, which is often the case, she arranges the appointment, attends the appointment with her client, has her client write a check to pay for these specialized services, and then oversees the entire process. In effect, she views herself as the "watcher" between her client and any specialist involved.

Everyone is happy. Amy is focused on her ideal clientele. Her centers-of-influence have become ongoing sources of introductions and referrals, and her specialists love her. Because of her background in law, she is determined to expand her knowledge regarding estate planning and taxes. Her lessons are biweekly lunches with her strategic alliance partners. She gives them a lot of business and all she wants to do is expand her basic knowledge, not become an expert. Her expertise is in managing the relationships, knowing how to identify problems and knowing where to go for the solution.

Mastering the 8 Key Financial Advisory Categories, even on a Team basis, can be overwhelming if you attempt it alone. Taking a chapter from Amy's success story, you will discover that it's easier than you might have anticipated because you now have a strategy with specific steps to follow.

Your strategy is to close the gap between what you know and can do now and what you need to know and do, in order to build a successful *21st Century Financial Practice™* that will provide complex financial solutions for your affluent clientele. The only thing left is to do it! Plan what you will do, and then do what you plan.

Designing an Effective
Financial Advisory Process

---

*Order and simplification are the first
steps toward the mastery of a subject*
Thomas Mann

I n the midst of this book project I was asked to do a favor
for a friend of a friend; a broker my client friend had
trained with some 30 years earlier, and who was now
asking for guidance in developing a Team. He was considering the son of his close friend, a 32 year-old young man with
an Ivy League MBA. What really aroused my interest was this
young man's role as a "relationship manager," working in
the high net worth division of a major bank in their city.

Beyond doing a favor for a friend, I jumped at the opportunity to get a face-to-face feeling for the fit between the two
disciplines: a traditional stockbroker and a high net worth
relationship manager. When the three of us met, I was not
disappointed.

The veteran stockbroker had developed an admirable
one-dimensional business with over 2,000 clients. He was
producing just over $1 million and earning nearly $500,000
annually. He certainly had created a wonderful life for him-
self by buying and selling stocks and bonds in the context of
the old sales and marketing model of Wall Street.

In contrast, our young high net worth MBA was manag-
ing the relationships of only 50 households. His minimum
account size was $10 million, and he was controlling nearly
$1 billion of investable assets for his bank. As I walked both
of them through my 21st Century Financial Practice™
as a model they should consider when building a Wealth
Management Team, the young MBA confirmed what I had
expected, "This is exactly what I do at the bank. It's all pro-
cess, except yours appears to be even more complete." The
compliment was appreciated, but the "it's all process" state-
ment was especially important. The young man went on to
explain how easy working with wealthy people really is if you
simply manage the relationship and adhere to a process. He
later revealed that most of his clients considered the bank to
be rather cold, but they liked him.

Although they could become a powerful complement of
traditional stockbroker and high net worth relationship man-
ager, they were miles apart. The broker offered an opportu-
nity for this young banker to earn considerably more money
(he was making less than $200,000) and never again have
his career dependent on the whims of a large bank. On the
other hand, the risk was tremendous. This old school broker
had no concept of process. I left them with some work to com-
plete, work that would hopefully assist them in determining
whether or not there would be a fit from a human perspective.
From a business perspective, their potential was unlimited.

The web site *www.moneyconcepts.com* features a list of "8 convincing
reasons why people need an Independent Financial Planner." One of those
reasons describes a process that clearly demonstrates why Financial Planners have been so successful.

An Independent Financial Planner makes it his or her business to learn who you are, where you are with your investment program and where you want to go. From this "getting to know you" process, your planner can offer customized strategies for retirement planning, increasing after-tax yields, funding your children's education, and planning for your parents financial needs in their later years.

www.moneyconcepts.com

Your Financial Advisory efforts must also begin with an effective "getting to know you" process that accomplishes an important task while avoiding one of the problems financial professionals often create for themselves. Your *task* is to use an interview process to discover four important things about your client's level of emotional involvement in their financial matters. What you *must avoid* is overwhelming them with the technical jargon of your profession. You need to gather critical information, not try to impress them with what you know. You build trust with Affluent Investors through quality face-to-face interactions. There is no other way.

The "Getting to Know You" Process

Because this "getting to know you" process is so important to your future relationship with each client, we will begin this chapter with an indepth explanation of how to conduct this interview. Following are the four things, in sequence, that you want to discover.

1. **Sources of Wealth**. You should ask them to describe in general terms (rather than very specific numbers) what income they receive presently and expect to receive in the future.

   As they describe that income for you, make notes in the same categories used when you created your *Ideal Client Profile* in Chapter 4.

- *Generated Wealth* – achieved through their personal enterprise.

- *Earned Wealth* – received as an employee.

- *Received Wealth* – received through retirement, stock options, divorce, or inheritance.

If they have their own business and receive salary and benefits, you may want to separate that (earned wealth) from wealth they receive as profits, etc. (generated wealth). Don't worry about specific numbers at this point. They probably won't have all the documents they need – and you will want to investigate those documents later to make certain the numbers you have are accurate. In each category, ask and make notes on their *present* and *future* sources of income.

2. **Goals and Priorities in Their Use of Wealth**. Note that the 20 descriptions below are void of technical terminology. There are three reasons for this. First is to avoid embarrassing your client by forcing them to ask what it means. Second, and equally important, is to avoid any misunderstanding that comes from assuming what a term means. You know the technical definition; they may know a "street" definition that doesn't include everything it should. Third, the statements will enable you to focus on the purpose behind financial products, not the products themselves.

We recommend following this procedure.

- Read an item.

- Ask if it is a *goal* – and write *yes or no* based on their response. If they can't decide, use a question mark (?).

- If it *is* a goal, ask whether they view it as a *High, Medium, or Low Priority* – and write their response.

Then continue, one item at a time. You may also want to make notes about *how* they respond to specific items. This is a great opportunity to discover how they really feel about their finances. Here are the suggested categories.

Obligations

- To meet their current financial obligations to creditors (monthly bills and payments).

- To reduce debt (which cannot be paid off in the current month).

- To eliminate debt within ___ months (fill in).

Lifestyle

- To maintain their current lifestyle.

- To upgrade their current lifestyle within ___ months (fill in).

- To provide for future financial security – to never be reliant on others.

Budget and Net Worth

- To always have a current understanding of their net worth (the value of what they have minus what they owe).

- To budget what they have coming in and how they use it to pay expenses.

Taxes

- To pay taxes on time.

- To minimize the amount of taxes they pay.

Insurance

- To insure against serious financial loss due to medical bills and/or not being able to work.

- To insure against serious financial loss from having to replace or repair damage to their home, vehicles, and other real estate and large tangible property investments.

Education

- To pay for their children's present private school education.

- To pay for their own or their spouse's degree completion over the next ____ (fill in) years.

- To financially support _____ % (fill in) of their children's post high school education.

- To financially support _____ % (fill in) of _____ (fill in) post high school education.

Retirement

- To retire by the age of _____ (fill in) which occurs in _____ years (fill in).

- To retire with at least _____ % (fill in) of their current level of income for at least _____ (fill in) years.

Estate

- To have a detailed plan of how and to whom their property, valuables, and money will be distributed upon their death.

Giving

- To have a Charitable Giving Plan that is consistent with their values and compatible with the rest of their financial needs, goals, and priorities.

3. **Present Efforts to Manage, Preserve, Create, and Distribute Wealth**. In contrast to Item 2, technical terms can be used here. If Affluent Investors have any of these financial tools or products, they will have some understanding of what they are. If they don't, they may ask what it is and you can use the description from the goals and priorities in Item 2 to explain.

If their answer for a tool or product is *yes*, ask for a general description – and take notes. As with the Sources of Wealth (Item 1), you will look at the actual documents later to extract the exact information. The following should be included:

- Budget

- Cash Flow Budget

- Net Worth Statement

- Life Insurance

- Disability Insurance

- Health Insurance

- Property and Casualty Insurance

- Savings

- Tax Planning

- Retirement Planning

- Personal Investments

- Business Expansion

- Education Planning

- Charitable Giving

- Estate Planning

4. **Risk Tolerance**. Many brokerage firms use quizzes to assess a person's tolerance for risk. We recommend that you resist that approach. Affluent Investors typically do not appreciate answering questions when they don't know exactly what the intent and meaning of that question is. You may already have a more direct way to uncover risk tolerance. If so, use it.

   If not, start by simply asking, "When you invest for future returns, what are you more concerned with?"

   a. Protecting the money that you invested?

   b. Risking those funds to receive the highest possible return?

   c. Somewhere in between?

   If they respond with "somewhere in between," probe further to see which direction they are leaning – and how far toward that end of the continuum.

   This "getting to know you" information, gathered in this manner, will establish you as a professional. Consider it your "real time" version of what high net worth advisors successfully employ to provide solutions while managing the relationship with their wealthy clientele. You will find that this interview will provide you with a solid foundation for shaping a relationship of trust with your clients as you use this information to select and explain the solutions you recommend.

Obviously, you can adapt this line of questioning to fit your needs. The secret is being disciplined enough to make it part of your process. Once you have an effective interview process established, you will be ready for the *Financial Advisory Process* itself. Keep in mind that you don't have to be the expert in all the areas covered, but you do need to become the quarterback of all the solutions.

Your Financial Advisory Process

Understanding the term "process" is vital for your success. Financial advising and planning is not an event. Nor is it merely a series of events that occur as you determine, "Oh, yeah. I almost forgot. We need to ..."

Process is "a natural phenomenon marked by gradual changes that lead toward a particular result." (Merriam-Webster Dictionary, 1997) Each phrase in that definition says something important about creating a sequential *Financial Advisory Process*.

- *Natural phenomenon* – Your process must be real, not artificial. It must guide your activity in a way that works for you, and for your client. When presented to your client, it has to make perfect sense to them.

- *Marked by gradual changes* – You will be suggesting that your clients change their habits and even their attitudes toward managing their finances. That change can happen only if it is evolutionary, not revolutionary. The steps of your process must be designed for gradual change. Each step must be a natural extension of the previous step and be adequate preparation for the next step.

- *That lead toward a particular result* – You need to help your clients establish clear goals early enough in the process so that you and they are pulled toward those goals and feel that pull each step of the way. For that to happen those goals must be their goals (not yours), and they must be consistent with their values, needs and desires. The "getting to know you" interview process is designed to help you achieve exactly that.

Your challenge now is to design a sequential *Financial Advisory Process* that has both the structure and flexibility to meet the needs of each client and be workable for you. As you design that *process*, we suggest that you define it as a series of face-to-face meetings with your client. For *each meeting*, you will need to define the following.

1. *Objectives* for the meeting – stated in terms of outcomes. What needs to be accomplished by the end of this meeting?

2. *Activity Agenda* – steps to accomplish these objectives, including:

   • Questions to ask the client.

   • Questions the client will possibly ask you (be prepared).

3. *Competency* required to successfully complete this session.

   • *Knowledge* – knowing what questions to ask, answers to give, options to suggest, and advice to offer.

   • *Skills* – being able to Profile, Educate, Analyze, Solve, Implement, and Monitor competently (see Chapter 7).

4. What *assignments* to make in order to build a bridge to the next face-to-face meeting. Both you and your client should have specific tasks to be completed by your next meeting, which will ensure that your meetings are connected. What you and your client do between meetings is what links the meetings together.

5. No later than the next day, prepare a *written Meeting Report* and send a copy to your client. The report should include:

- What was covered and decisions that were made.

- Assignments – yours and theirs.

- Next Milestone Meeting – the date and time, or circumstances that will determine when a meeting is appropriate.

At an early, appropriate point in your *Financial Advisory Process*, I highly recommend creating a Financial Organizer for each client. This is a loose-leaf binder you provide to each client as a convenient means of storing all documentation relating to the development and implementation of agreed upon solutions for the multidimensional aspects of their personal finances. Think in terms of adding value by a creating a personal Day Timer or Franklin Planner for your clientele's financial affairs.

Brilliant in its down-to-earth practicality, the Financial Organizer is a simple method for quantifying, demonstrating, and communicating value. Used properly, it can serve as the platform upon which you reposition yourself in the mind of your clientele. In case you find yourself procrastinating regarding the development and implementation of this tool as an integral part of your practice, consider Mary's story.

> *Mary, a veteran advisor, put it off for six months before being persuaded by her Assistant to give it a try. Upon Mary's agreement, her Assistant proceeded to compile data, organize statements, and create a professional looking Financial Organizer for five select clients that they had earmarked as having upgrade potential.*
>
> *Using the Financial Organizer as her upgrading platform, Mary was able to uncover and bring in an additional $2.4 million from her four targeted clients. Equally impor-*

tant, she was so successful in repositioning her value that three of the four provided her with a total of five quality referrals.

Thanks to her forward thinking Assistant, Mary was also armed with appointment cards and concluded each meeting by scheduling a 20-minute conference call for a specified date the following quarter. Each client departed with his or her Financial Organizer and appointment card in hand. In one meeting Mary was able to reposition her value in the minds of her clients. And let me repeat, the Financial Organizer served as the platform enabling this scenario to unfold as a professional, value-added, contact.

Financial Organizer suggested binder tabs.

Tab 1:   Our Financial Advisory Process

Tab 2:   Your Financial Plan

Tab 3:   Ongoing Review – Milestone Meetings

- Meeting Reports

Tab 4:   Budgeting and Cash Flow Management

- 12-Month Budget

- 12-Month Cash Flow Budget

Tab 5:   Net Worth Statement

Tab 6:   Insurance

- Life & Health

- Property & Casualty

Tab 7:   Investments

- Stocks

- Mutual Fund

- Bonds

Tab 8:   Education Plan

Tab 9:   Tax Information

Tab 10:   Retirement Plan

Tab 11:   Estate Plan

Tab 12:   Charitable Giving Plan

Your final step in designing your *Financial Advisory Process* is to identify the specific steps you will take a client through – and the objectives you will seek to achieve at each step.

The steps below are adapted from a 6-step process recommended by International Certified Financial Planners (ICFP). They may work well for you, as long as you build adequate bridges between them. You may have another approach. The key is to define the *Financial Advisory Process* that works best for you. Mary already was a CFP, but hadn't fully capitalized on her credentials because she wasn't always disciplined in following her process. Remember, *process* is the key to attracting, servicing, and retaining the affluent. If anything, the following should give you an indication of how simple it can be.

Step 1: Establish and define client-planner relationship

Objectives:

1. Explain the overall financial process plus concepts and issues appropriate to this individual.

2. Explain (or document) the services to be provided.

3. Define the client's responsibilities as well as yours.

4. Explain how you will be compensated, and by whom.

5. Agree with the client on how long the professional relationship should last.

6. Agree on how decisions will be made.

Step 2: Gather client data, including goals

Objectives:

1. Obtain information about their financial situation (resources and obligations) through interviewing and questionnaires.

2. Work with them to define their personal and financial needs, priorities, and goals.

3. Determine their time frame for results and discuss.

4. Define their values, attitudes, expectations, and their feelings about risk.

5. Hold off giving any advice until all the necessary records and documents are collected.

   Note: Step 2 builds from and formalizes the information gathered during your "getting to know you" interview.

Step 3:   Analyze and evaluate client's financial status

Objectives:

1. Analyze the records and documents provided and organize the information. Identify any problem areas or opportunities with respect to the 8 Key Financial Advisory Categories.

2. Determine what they can and should do to meet their goals, and formulate your financial planning recommendations for each of the 8 Key Financial Advisory Categories.

Step 4:   Develop and present financial planning recommendations and/or alternatives (the Financial Plan)

Objectives:

1. Offer financial planning recommendations that address their goals, based on the information they provided.

2. Help them understand those recommendations so they can make informed decisions.

3. Listen to their concerns and revise your recommendations as appropriate.

4. Complete a formal Financial Plan and present it to the client.

Step 5:   Implement financial planning recommendations

Objectives:

1. Develop a working agreement as to how the recommendations (Plan) will be carried out.

2. Determine specifically:

   • What your Wealth Management Team (Team
   Members or contracted services) will do, and
   the designated person who will be coordinating
   and reporting to the client.

   • What the client will do, with the designated
   person serving as their "coach" each step of the
   way.

3. Establish milestones when progress to date will be
reviewed with the client.

Step 6:   Monitor financial planning recommendations

Objectives:

1. Agree with your client on a monitoring and accountability system that will ensure the client that:

   • Everything is being accomplished according to
   plan.

   • Each accomplished task is helping the client
   move successfully toward their goals.

   • Changes in tax laws, economic circumstances,
   the client's personal or financial status, etc. are
   being identified and reported to the client.

2. Meet with the client.

- At milestone points to update.

- At any point where changes in the tax laws, economic conditions, the client's personal or financial status, etc. require new decisions.

With the development of your "getting to know you" interview procedure and your formal *Financial Advisory Process*, your Wealth Management Team will be transformed into a 21st century business enterprise. To ensure that everything you do to attract, qualify, close, interview, and advise new Affluent Investor clients continually adds value to that relationship, you need to make certain that you have a highly efficient operation.

In the next section, you will learn how to plan and implement the *Operational Efficiency Process* of your *21st Century Financial Practice™*. Here you will make certain that everyone on your Team has a clearly defined role within delegated Areas of Responsibility, to ensure that you can deliver on your *Financial Advisory Process*.

The
Operational Efficiency
Process

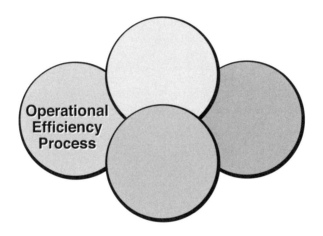

Chapter 9
Defining Operational Efficiency

Chapter 10
Delegating for Operational Efficiency

Chapter 11
Developing Your Team to
Achieve Operational Efficiency

Chapter 12
Documenting Operational Efficiency

Defining
Operational Efficiency

"We are Ladies and Gentlemen
Serving Ladies and Gentlemen."
Ritz-Carlton Motto

This is a tale involving two different clients, one a consultant and the other a doctor. Two Financial Advisors play the lead roles in this story. One is in the midst of developing a Wealth Management Team under the umbrella of the *21st Century Financial Practice™*. The other continues to operate solo as a one-dimensional stockbroker.

Each Financial Advisor received an urgent request from their client to have a check in the neighborhood of $14,000 drawn on their account for the purchase of a used car. Each client had a daughter graduating from high school – similar requests, but with two different outcomes. Both Financial Advisors recognized the request as doable and urgent, but their solutions and outcomes were as different as night and day.

The one-dimensional stockbroker placed his client's request in written form on his Assistant's "to-do" pile; an Assistant he shared with another broker. Unfortunately the request got lost amidst the large stack of other "to-do's".

139

They didn't discuss it, and no priority status was attached to the request. As you might imagine, the Assistant viewed the request as simply another one of the many daily tasks the two brokers gave her.

The client called the next afternoon, insisted on speaking with the broker, and told him in no uncertain terms, "I guess I'm not a big enough client to have this simple request attended to in a prompt manner. Please close my account as I will never do business with you or anyone else as unprofessional as you again." A $2.7 million account was closed before the original request was rescued from yesterday's stack of "to-do's". Ugh.

The second request was handled very differently. In the process of forming a Wealth Management Team, the second Advisor had eliminated the practice of assigning daily tasks with a system of defining Areas of Responsibility for which individual Team Members would be responsible. Even more important, all responsibilities had one focus – serving clients quickly and efficiently. Because of that, the request went to the right person and was processed immediately.

Because of the urgency, the check was hand delivered before noon. Receiving the request, processing the account, and delivering the check could easily have been passed on from person-to-person before the Team was formed. Did the Team get all kinds of kudos for a job well done? Not really. This was expected behavior in response to a reasonable request. Did this Wealth Management Team demonstrate and communicate their value by their actions? Absolutely! Will this level of service stimulate word-of-mouth influence within the centers-of-influence of this affluent client? You bet they will!

This real-life story illustrates the contrast between responsibility-based *Operational Efficiency* and task-based operational dysfunction. Very few affluent clients will tolerate the latter. *Operational Efficiency* is the lubricant that makes your engine function as advertised. When not properly attended to, automobile engines quickly wear out and die. In the world of wealth management, as the one-dimensional broker in our story quickly discovered, not properly attending to affluent clients also spells death to an account.

Efficiency is a relatively simple concept. It essentially refers to how well resources are used to produce a given output. If you can reduce the time and resources used to produce a product or service, you have increased efficiency. Improving efficiency can be a wonderful thing. However, it can also become the primary reason you are losing clients.

Because emphasis on efficiency naturally encourages an inward focus, it's easy to get caught up in doing things to improve operations while completely ignoring your clients. This has been prevalent in the financial services industry where processes, procedures, and forms are too often created for the convenience of the company, not the client.

To offset this "big mistake," management and quality experts have introduced another e-word into our vocabulary: *effectiveness*, which quality improvement guru H. James Harrington defines as "how well customer expectations are met." Now we have two concepts, both beginning with the letter 'e,' and each pulling us in totally opposite directions. Each becomes the password to access the kind of myopic thinking that drags organizations down. Marketing wants us to improve our *effectiveness*, while the administrative and operations folks strive for *efficiency*. That impasse results in stagnation and you cannot afford this kind of divided thinking within your Team operations.

Everything we have presented to you thus far has focused on becoming more *effective* in attracting, servicing, and retaining affluent clients who match your *Ideal Client Profile*. The next four chapters on the *Operational Efficiency Process* will enhance that emphasis, not reverse it. Efficiency must not be allowed to become an end in itself. To keep that from happening, we need to be clear about what we mean by Operational Efficiency.

Operational Efficiency Defined

Until now, you have focused on doing the right things.

- Being continually pulled ahead by your 5-Year Business Plan.

- Using Metrics Scorecards to monitor your progress.

- Networking your way into the lives of Affluent Investors who match your *Ideal Client Profile*.

- Broadening the number and type of financial solutions you offer.

- Following a well-defined yet flexible *Financial Advisory Process* to service clients.

These are the *right things* that make you effective as a 21st Century Wealth Management Team. It's critical that efforts to improve Operational Efficiency complement and enhance what you are doing, rather than compete with it. To help you achieve that goal, we will define *efficiency* as the *effort to reduce and eliminate waste.*

You become more efficient by reducing time spent and materials used, by eliminating delays and errors, by ensuring that your client's time is never wasted, and by making certain that every Team Member's talent and potential is fully and efficiently utilized. At the same time, nothing that adds value for a client should be considered as waste, even if it requires additional time, materials, or effort in order to achieve the quality required to meet that client's expectations. You must always go the extra mile to serve a client. Once you have done that, you can look for ways to maintain the same quality level in a more efficient manner (i.e., in less time with reduced resources).

In order for this to happen, everyone on your Team must become "Kaizen conscious." Masaaki Imai defines Kaizen as "gradual, unending improvement; doing little things better; setting and achieving ever-higher standards." The following chart, which contrasts the features of Kaizen and Innovation may help you to clarify your new strategy.

	Kaizen	**Innovation**
1. Effort	Long-term & long-lasting	Short-term, but dramatic
2. Pace	Small steps	Big steps
3. Time Frame	Continuous and incremental	Intermittent and non-incremental
4. Change	Gradual and constant	Abrupt and volatile
5. Involvement	Everybody	Select "experts"
6. Mode	Maintain and improve	Scrap and rebuild
7. Effort	By people	Through technology
8. Evaluation Focus	The process and effort to achieve better results	The results alone

Adapted from : *KAIZEN, The Key to Japan's Success* (Imai 1986)

The *21st Century Financial Practice™* model requires a significant paradigm shift, a whole new way of thinking about and doing financial advising. Making this paradigm shift is your first big challenge. It requires innovation. But once you have made that shift, it will be ongoing improvement involving every Team Member all of the time, that will be your key to success.

As you look around, you will increasingly find other Wealth Management Teams (your competition!) struggling with that paradigm shift and learning to do many of the "right things" we have recommended. Doing those right things efficiently is what will help to set you apart and cause others to wonder how you gained a competitive edge so quickly. You will have done it by becoming operationally efficient, but you won't tell them that!

Let me share the entire Ritz-Carlton Credo to stimulate your thinking.

Ritz-Carlton Credo

The Ritz-Carlton Hotel is a place where the genuine care and comfort of our guests is our highest mission.

We pledge to provide the finest personal service and facilities for our guests who will always enjoy a warm, relaxed, yet refined ambience.

The Ritz-Carlton experience enlivens the senses, instills well-being, and fulfills even the unexpressed wishes and needs of our guests.

Affluent travelers typically have their favorite Ritz-Carlton story. If you are committed to serving the same clientele with the same level of excellence, you must define your Operational Efficiency as clearly as the Ritz-Carlton does.

We will consider four D's in the *Operational Efficiency Process*: define, delegate, develop and document. In this chapter, we consider the first D, *Define*. Here your Team will work together to define the following three aspects of your operation:

- Areas of Responsibility

- Performance Results

- Time Wasters

Defining Areas of Responsibility

Doing tasks and assigning tasks to others is not enough to achieve Operational Efficiency. It's too easy to perform a task without giving any thought to why you're doing it and how it connects to and impacts the overall efficiency of your operation.

Connection and *impact* are the primary reasons for moving away from tasks and reorganizing around clearly defined Areas of Responsibility. *Tasks* are closed-ended. They have beginning and ending points, and once ended we tend to forget about them – even if they are repeated. *Responsibilities* are open-ended, so accountability is stronger and several inter-related tasks are often involved. Greater connection and impact are the obvious benefits.

This involves a reorganizing process, which includes the following three steps.

1. **List Current Tasks**. Have *every* Team Member prepare a list of all the tasks they perform during a normal week, whether they have been assigned those tasks or simply do them because they need to be done. Everyone should also note whether they perform each task daily, weekly, monthly, when asked to, etc. The purpose is to have a comprehensive list of Team tasks that can be reorganized into Areas of Responsibilities.

2. **Redistribute Current Tasks by Areas of Responsibility**. When we work with Wealth Management Teams, we typically recommend using the following four Areas of Responsibility.

145

a. **Business Development (BD)**

Focus: Attract new Ideal Clients by:

- Defining and researching market segments.

- Connecting with, qualifying, and closing prospects.

- Managing a Referral Network.

- Managing a Referral Alliance System.

- Managing the weekly and quarterly Metrics Scorecards.

b. **Operations (OPN)**

Focus: Coordinate the *Financial Advisory Process* steps by:

- Preparing the clients' *Financial Organizer* binders.

- Setting up client meetings.

- Preparing for client meetings.

- Preparing and sending out meeting reports.

- Completing assignments between client meetings.

c. **Service (SVC)**

Focus: Ensure that clients and Team Members have what they need, where and when they need it, by:

- Handling clients' questions, complaints, and requests for information.

- Making certain each Team Member can efficiently perform his or her tasks.

d. **Administration (ADM)**

Focus: Support the other Areas of Responsibility, plus keep current with inner-company requirements, by:

- Organizing and maintaining a filing system for client records, etc.

- Ordering and maintaining office supplies, forms, etc.

- Handling inner-company reports, correspondence, complaints, etc.

Go through each Team Member's list of tasks and place the appropriate letter abbreviations (BD, OPN, SVC, or ADM) in front of each task to indicate the Area of Responsibility to which it should be assigned.

When developing your *21st Century Metrics System* back in Chapter 5, you were asked to create a list of Fixed Daily Activities, or FDAs. Go back and review that list to make certain no task has been overlooked here.

3. **Finalize the Areas of Responsibility**.

a. Develop a separate worksheet for each Area of Responsibility. Include the following for each.

- The *description* from No. 2, above.

- The list of *tasks* assigned to that Area – indicating the Team Member(s) who presently carry out each Task.

b. Review each Area of Responsibility worksheet and add any additional tasks that you feel are needed.

You may be thinking that simply reorganizing tasks by Areas of Responsibility doesn't go far enough, and you're right. Once you are confident that these lists contain everything they should at this point, set them aside. You will return to them in Chapter 10.

Defining Performance Results

You will know that you have Operational Efficiency when, as a Wealth Management Team, you consistently produce the Ritz-Carlton and FedEx type of *results* clients expect. Even though each client has their own unique set of expectations, they tend to fall into four categories with specific standards they want you to meet.

Performance Results

Performance expectations in terms of *Quality*

- Everything is done right the first time.
- Everything is clear and understandable to the client.
- Clients always receive knowledgeable and helpful assistance from your Team

Performance expectations in terms of *Convenience*

- Everything is delivered when and where the client needs or wants it.
- Promises are always kept.

Performance expectations in terms of *Personalization*

- Everything is customized to each client's unique needs and wants.
- You continually find helpful new ways to serve each client in a personal way.

Performance expectations in terms of *Cost*

- The client perceives that the value you provide justifies the fees they pay you.

- Your value-added services are continually reducing the client's "cost" in terms of time, effort, and dollars.

Your challenge is to *perform* at a level that meets or exceeds those expectations. That's why we call them *Performance Results*. Catchy sayings and motivational talks about performance are not enough. You need to define and measure the results you want to achieve.

These are serious expectations, so how do you prepare yourselves as a Wealth Management Team to provide the Performance Results that will meet those expectations? It's a whole lot easier to do that when you are working alone – assuming you have the desire and expertise to do it. Approaching this from a Team standpoint is a different matter. You need to work together as a Team to establish a set of *Performance Standards* that you all agree (with the emphasis on "all agree") will enable you to collectively produce the Performance Results your clients expect.

As you begin your discussion together, it's important to gain acceptance and commitment to the principle behind setting these standards.

You are determined to become a world class Wealth Management Team that can match Ritz-Carlton service and FedEx efficiency – and will blow the competition out of the water, even those who offer the same range of services that you provide.

Performance Standards are especially important in the following two areas:

1. **Client Contacts**

- *Client Contact Responsibility.* The individual who initiates or receives a client contact of any type automatically becomes totally responsible for managing that contact until it is concluded to the complete satisfaction of the client. Never again will anyone on your Team tell a client that they need to call someone else – or even that you will have someone else call them. The Team Member who made the initial contact manages every situation emerging from that client contact. *Managing* includes contacting the appropriate people to get answers and solve any problems involved. There must be no exceptions to this *Performance Standard.*

- *Response Time.* When responding to client-initiated contacts, you need to establish specific response times for phone calls (number of rings) and for faxes, e-mails, and postal mail (maximum number of hours). Once established, those response times must be monitored. If you find you cannot respond quickly enough, you need to adjust what you do in order to meet those standards – not adjust the standards to what you are doing.

- *Other.* As you discuss client contacts, you will probably identify other areas where *Performance Standards* can be set to ensure the optimum level of service and efficiency.

2. **Financial Advisory Process**

You also need to define *Performance Standards* for each step in your *Financial Advisory Process.* This will require some serious thought and effort, and you may want to assign specific process steps to the Team Members who know those areas best. Ask them to draft suggestions for the Team to consider. You can use the four Performance Expectations (Quality, Convenience, Personalization, and Cost) as benchmarks for exploring each process step. The question is:

What Performance Standards should we define to ensure that we provide the level of performance our clients expect in terms of quality, convenience, personalization, and cost?

Setting *Performance Standards* is the easy part. Adhering to those standards will only happen if you establish some system for monitoring your performance. Self-monitoring is best, but it only works when every Team Member is committed to the standards themselves. Make certain that commitment is there. Then have each Team Member develop a worksheet to self-monitor the standards that pertain to him or her. That worksheet should be used for at least 30 days – or until you are all convinced that the standards have become a natural and integral part of your daily performance.

Defining and Eliminating Time Wasters

Being efficient with your time does not mean you must always be doing something. Time to plan, to think, to celebrate, and even to just relax should be factored into your efficient use of time.

As with the other two areas under *define*, this is an excellent Team Building opportunity. Your sense of teamwork should be well enough established by this point that you can encourage honest responses from each Team Member. The goal is to identify and help each other reduce Time Wasters so that overall Team efficiency is enhanced. There are two parts to this Time Wasters exercise:

1. The first is done with the entire Team present. Using the common Time Wasters listed below, have each Team Member go through the list individually and note which ones they presently experience.

    *   Interruptions – telephone or in person.

    *   Meetings that are poorly planned and led.

    *   Assigned a task, but not sure what to do.

    *   Assigned a task, but don't know how to do it.

- Unsure about priorities – everything is presented as a crisis.

- Attempting to do too much – unrealistic time estimates.

- Having trouble saying "no".

- Indecision and procrastination.

- Cluttered desk – personal disorganization.

- Failing to plan and organize your day.

- Conflict – causing a communication breakdown.

- Lack of self-discipline.

- Feeling tired.

Then discuss each item, ending up with a strategy to reduce or help others to reduce each one. For example, let's say that two Team Members are experiencing too many interruptions and the discussion reveals that most of those interruptions are by other Team Members. If you have a strong commitment to improving Team efficiency (reducing waste), it should be easy to work out a strategy to relieve that situation.

2. The second part is done individually, and then reviewed as a Team. Each Team Member should develop a worksheet with three columns entitled as follows.

- *Time Waster* – a description.

- *Why* it occurs.

- *How* I will eliminate it.

When you come together to discuss these worksheets, you will have a glimpse of the inner workings of your Team. The "*How* I will eliminate it" will tell you how realistic each solution is, and what kind of support is needed to ensure success. The network of support you create will be a key factor in improving Team coordination and communication.

The last and very important part of eliminating Time Wasters is to meet as a Team in 30 days to discuss your progress. Equally important in your effort to reduce Time Wasters is your progress toward becoming a highly effective and efficient Team.

You have now defined Areas of Responsibility, Performance Standards, and Time Wasters. You are also monitoring progress toward meeting Performance Standards and working together to reduce those Time Wasters. This is where *Kaizen consciousness* needs to kick in. As we move on in Chapter 10 to the second "D", *Delegate*, you will find that Operational Efficiency is not an event or even a series of events. It's an ongoing, never-ending effort by everyone to do things better today than they were done yesterday. If and when that happens, Operational Efficiency will become a reality, you will have developed your own Wealth Management Team credo, and your competition will be constantly scrambling to catch up. It doesn't get much better than that!

10

Delegating
Operational Efficiency

*Give me a smart idiot
over a stupid genius any day.*

Samuel Goldwyn

The two Financial Advisors in the tale at the beginning of Chapter 9 provide an important contrast regarding the art of delegation. Although they may sound similar, there's a dramatic difference between delegating tasks and delegating responsibilities.

As a management concept, *delegation* has been around a long time. Much has been written about it, but few have learned to use it effectively. If not done in the context of mastering Operational Efficiency, delegation is a lost cause. That's particularly true if you plan to work with the affluent because they will not tolerate it if you allow tasks to fall through the cracks; and handing a task off to someone else increases the risk of that happening.

To delegate successfully, you must entrust responsibility to another person – which means you are committing that responsibility to them with confidence. Which is exactly what you're asking your affluent clients to do with you; and as noted in the Introduction to this book, Financial Advisors have a "lack of confidence" issue to overcome. If you will recall, the three largest performance expectation gaps reported by Affluent Investors in our study were:

- Not receiving satisfactory value for the fees and/or commissions paid.

- Not trusting the quality of the financial advice received.

- Not trusting that financial advice received is always in their best interest.

Delegating responsibilities to one another within your Wealth Management Team has a direct correlation to your ability to eliminate these performance gap perceptions. If you cannot entrust responsibility to each other with confidence, your Performance Results in terms of Quality, Convenience, Personalization, and Cost will not meet, let alone exceed, client expectations.

Delegating tasks is relatively simple, if you communicate properly and inspect what you expect. Tasks have a starting and ending point, and they are typically short-term. They are easy to monitor and the risk factor is low. The problem is, that it often takes more time to delegate and monitor the results than to do the task yourself. Delegating responsibilities is an entirely different matter, and that's your challenge here.

At this point, you should have the worksheets that were developed in Chapter 9 for each of the four Areas of Responsibility.

- *Business Development* (BD) – attracting new clients.

- *Operations* (OPN) – coordinating the *Financial Advisory Process* steps.

- *Service* (SVC) – ensuring that clients and Team Members have what they need, where and when they need it.

- *Administration* (ADM) – supporting the other Areas of Responsibility, plus keeping current with inner-company requirements.

Each worksheet should include:

- A *description* of the particular Area of Responsibility.

- A list of all the *tasks* that Team Members perform in that area, including the name of the Team Member who performs each task. These were extracted from the list of tasks created by each Team Member.

You will want to keep these worksheets in front of you as you read through this next section.

Delegation Guidelines

We will approach this section from the standpoint of the Wealth Management Team Leader, typically the Senior Financial Advisor on the Team.

Inability to delegate is a common problem of leadership. As a Team Leader, possible reasons that you prefer not to delegate might be that:

- You are used to working independently and feel more comfortable doing tasks than supervising the work of others.

- You are not familiar enough with the skills of other Team Members and are therefore unsure of their ability to take on more responsibility.

- You hate correcting other people's work.

- You simply feel you can do some things better than others.

There are two critical questions each leader must answer about delegation.

1. **How Much Responsibility**? Competent people want to know the specific responsibilities that are being delegated to them. It's much easier to know how much responsibility when specific tasks are delegated,

and a person is responsible for completing a particular task by a specific date. Delegating Business Development, Operations, Service, and Administration Areas of Responsibility will stretch the "How much?" question much further. To do that successfully, you need to be confident of three things:

- That each Area of Responsibility is completely and clearly defined.

- That the Team Members to whom each Area of Responsibility will be delegated are competent enough to meet the challenge.

- That the process by which Areas of Responsibility are defined and delegated achieves that assignment successfully.

2. **How Much Authority**? Authority is the fuel that makes responsibility happen. It boils down to determining the extent to which you will allow someone else to make decisions, especially those decisions that impact clients and/or require spending money.

Management Principles and Delegation

The following five management principles will help you delegate Areas of Responsibility and monitor performance.

1. **Participative Planning**. If all Team Members are involved in planning and organizing, it is more likely that they will buy into the results, making delegation easier. Having done that, following the steps below for delegating Areas of Responsibility will continue that level of involvement.

2. **Balancing Responsibility and Authority**. An important part of delegating is making clear the direction responsibility flows and who reports to whom. Equally important is to clearly define when permission to act is required, what decisions can be made by individuals and what decisions must be brought to the Team Leader.

3. **Managing By Exception**. Defining which decisions require permission and which do not, will not cover every possibility. It must be made clear that exceptions will occur, and that the full resources of the entire Team are at the disposal of any Team Member in those situations. They will come to you when they know permission is needed. They make decisions themselves when they are confident about making those decisions. Otherwise, they know they can cry "help" without any fear of recrimination.

4. **Consulting and Coaching**. Good Team Leaders know how other Team Members are doing. They learn that by visiting periodically with individuals over a cup of coffee; by holding timely and effective Team meetings; by asking the advice of Team Members who have the knowledge and experience to give that advice; or by helping Team Members when help is requested.

5. **Monitoring Performance**. This is a form of consulting and coaching, but it comes more from observing what people do, reviewing the results of their performance, and then intervening at the right time to ensure improvement. When someone's observed behavior or *Performance Results* indicate a problem, the following steps will be necessary.

  • Ask for an appointment with them, stating that there is a performance issue you want to discuss with them.

- Set a time and place when the meeting can be totally private and uninterrupted.

- Begin by clearly describing the problem. Tell them that your only goal is to work with them to solve that problem. Ask them if they agree that the problem exists.

- Next, describe the observed behavior or Performance Result that you believe is contributing to the problem. Make certain you do not attack them personally in any way. Focus specifically on their performance.

- Ask them if they agree with your assessment. This is a critical point. If necessary, repeat your goal of working with them to solve the problem and explain that you can't do that without knowing clearly what is causing the problem. Keep the discussion going, using give and take to come to agreement about the cause and their role in it.

- Ask them for solution options and present any others you feel should be considered.

- Discuss the options until you have agreed on a course of action.

- Define what will be done, by whom and when. Set a date for a follow-up meeting. Explain that the resources of the entire Team are at their disposal and that they should not hesitate to ask for help.

With the above guidelines established, you will be ready to call the Team together for the express purpose of delegating – of reorganizing your Team around the four Areas of Responsibility. Your goal is for your Team to emerge stronger than ever as a result of this exercise.

Delegating Areas of Responsibility

When you invite Team Members to this meeting, ask everyone to bring along their original list of tasks. At this momentous Team meeting, you will want to follow these steps.

1. Direct each Team Member to go through their personal task list and place a check mark in front of those tasks that they believe they perform well (do best). That is *do* best, not necessarily like best.

2. Together, go through the four Areas of Responsibility worksheets and have each Team Member place their initials in front of the same tasks that they checked off on their personal list. Don't be concerned if more than one individual places their initials in front of a given task.

   • If any Fixed Daily Activities (FDAs) have been added to an Area of Responsibility, discuss them and ask Team Members to place their initials in front of those that they believe they perform well.

3. Discuss each Area of Responsibility. Based on what various Team Members do best, as well as other insights and considerations, decide together which Team Member should take the *Lead Role* in each Area of Responsibility.

   Lead Role – This individual will have primary responsibility for coordinating all the activity (tasks) in that area. He or she is the "go to" person who makes certain that things are done efficiently, and that nothing falls through the cracks.

When selecting the person for the Lead Role, consider the following:

- In most cases, the Team Leader will take the Lead Role in the Business Development Area of Responsibility (BD). Upper-Middle Class and Affluent Investor clients identify with a person, not a Team. Most often that person is the senior member of the Team, the Team Leader.

- Make certain that the person in the Lead Role of the Operations Area of Responsibility is competent, experienced, process rather than task-oriented, and able to "connect" effectively with Upper-Middle Class and Affluent Investor clients.

4. Develop an *Area of Responsibility Profile* that includes the following information:

- **Title**. An example would be: *Business Development Area of Responsibility Profile*.

- **Focus**. Continuing the above example, it would be: *Attracting New Ideal Clients*.

- **Lead Role**. The name of the person assuming that role.

- **Tasks**. List the specific tasks for which the person in the Lead Role will be responsible.

- **Support Tasks / Assigned To**. List all the other tasks for that area and then select the individual(s) to be responsible for each and be sure to write down their name(s).

- **Potential Coordination Problems and What We Will Do to Prevent Them**. Discuss the potential coordination problems that could occur for each Area of Responsibility. Brainstorm what the person in the Lead Role as well as what other Team Members could do to prevent them. Make a list of preventive measures that make sense to all of you.

You have now accomplished the most challenging aspect of achieving Operational Efficiency; you have reorganized your Team. Change is taking place and you are working together to make it happen. Life will get even better!

Remember Mary and her Assistant who helped her to upgrade four clients? It was due to this exact process that her Assistant was able to convince Mary to use the Financial Organizers. If Mary had not delegated the entire responsibility of developing that powerful tool to her Assistant, the successful upgrade probably would not have happened.

Although there is no way to predict the exact results of committing to this process, it cannot help but be beneficial to your business. Agree to meet every 30 days as a Team to specifically discuss your progress with delegating Areas of Responsibility and specify that each Lead Role Team Member will be expected to give an honest appraisal.

You will find that change has occurred, but your Team's *Kaizen consciousness* will need to shift to an even higher level. You've only just begun; you have not arrived. Your ongoing, never-ending effort to do things better today than you did yesterday will be even more important now than ever before, as you move on to the third "D" in Chapter 11 and learn ways to *Develop* your Team in order to achieve *Operational Efficiency*.

Developing Your Team
To Achieve Operational Efficiency

You got to be careful
if you don't know where you're going
because you might not get there.

Yogi Berra

Y ou have already made two changes that make Team Member development absolutely essential. First is your reorganization around Areas of Responsibility. Gaining new knowledge and learning new skills will make an important contribution toward achieving the highest level of competency possible in each of the areas. Second is your commitment to Kaizen. Incremental improvement is nice to talk about, but improvement will not happen if people are not continually learning to do those things better.

Developing Your Team is receiving special attention in this book for two important reasons:

- Every individual on your Team has potential that remains untapped, regardless of how effective your Team development efforts have been up to this point. In fact, as each individual learns more, their potential expands exponentially.

- You can count on the fact that anyone you compete with for the affluent clients you want to attract, is not standing still. They are trying to improve as well. In your constantly changing business environment, individual development becomes your essential competitive edge strategy.

Most of the people you compete with will look toward new structures, new products, new services, new strategies, new anything, as a way to gain a competitive edge. Why? One reason is that it gives them something new to talk about. But you know that meeting expectations of affluent clients takes more than talk. It requires a competent, efficient Team of individuals who are continually developing new knowledge and skills in order to improve their performance. This approach to development has two key elements.

- Meeting the *Basic Development Needs* that are common to all Team Members.

- Helping each individual Team Member define and pursue *Individual Development Goals* relating to their Areas of Responsibility.

Meeting Basic Development Needs

Motivation theory has long suggested that our basic needs are arranged in a hierarchy. Abraham Maslow developed the best-known hierarchical need motivation theory in the 1950's, when he identified a five level need hierarchy. But a more recent version is Alderfer's ERG Theory, which narrows it down to the following three levels:

- *Existence Needs* (E) – the need for food, liquid, shelter, basic income, working conditions, etc. As these are satisfied, we tend to focus more on...

- *Relatedness Needs* (R) - the need for meaningful social and interpersonal relationships. As these are satisfied, we tend to focus more on...

- *Growth Needs* (G) – the need to make productive and creative contributions.

Besides the tendency to progress upward toward *Growth Needs*, Alderfer also identified what he called the *frustration-regression process*. If a person is continually frustrated with attempts to progress toward *Growth Needs*, he or she will redirect efforts to improve on a lower need category – focusing more on *Relatedness* or even *Existence Needs*. Engaging in idle conversation and constant complaints about compensation and benefits are indicators that frustration-regression is operative. (Ivancevich and Matteson 1996)

Although that's all helpful to know from a theoretical standpoint, Alderfer acknowledged that in reality, people focus on whatever needs they believe are not being met. You want your Team to focus on *growth*. When it comes to "growing" an effective Wealth Management Team, what every Team Member needs before anything else is to:

- Believe they *belong*.

- Have opportunities to *contribute*.

- Know they are *competent*.

- Be *recognized* and *rewarded*.

If you have been guiding your Team according to the game plan of this book, you have already begun the *Basic Development Needs* process, but you can probably do more. Since this is the foundation of Team Member development, it's important to be clear about what you are doing and what more you can do. So let's take inventory.

1. You have created a sense of *belonging* simply by making everyone a part of your Wealth Management Team. The question now is: Do they truly believe that they belong? By including them in discussing and refining Areas of Responsibility, setting Performance Standards, and

looking for ways to help each other reduce Time Wasters, you have taken a giant step in that direction.

What more can you do to make certain that everyone believes that they belong here?

2. You have begun empowering a sense of *competency* among Team Members by working to define what each individual does best, by building Areas of Responsibility around those competencies, and by assigning *Lead Roles.*

Was anyone "left out" in that process? What else can be done to identify and reinforce the competency that each Team Member brings to your Team?

3. You have ensured everyone's *contribution* in several ways, but most significantly by including the entire Team in making important decisions that impact your overall effectiveness. As you were working on Areas of Responsibility, you also made certain that everyone could contribute in at least one of those areas – and probably more.

Is there more you can you do to make certain that everyone knows daily that they are making a significant contribution to your Team's success?

4. You have also begun to *recognize* and *reward* achievement – by simply recognizing what they do best as the basis for assigning responsibility.

The major challenge is to make certain that recognition occurs at the right opportunity, and that each Team Member is rewarded for the right things in a fair and timely manner.

Your Recognition and Reward System

You are part of a system that has reviewed and rewarded performance almost solely on the basis of commissions generated from selling financial products. That has been your measure of success.

In Chapter 13, a new success measure, *client loyalty*, will be introduced. Production becomes a by-product of success in the *21st Century Financial Practice™* model, when you're no longer simply trying to sell financial products to anyone who will listen. Your focus is now on building a financial practice that attracts, services, and retains affluent clients. If you do that successfully, the dollars will come into your practice at levels you never imagined.

Because you and your fellow Team Members have been rewarded for sales activity, you have accordingly developed behavioral and attitudinal habits that need to end. You have now reorganized your Team according to Business Development, Operations, Service, and Administration Areas of Responsibility – all to better attract, service and retain affluent clients. You have established Performance Standards for client contacts, your *Financial Advisory Process,* and possibly other areas that you felt needed to be monitored. You've made an initial effort to reduce Time Wasters, and you have adopted a Kaizen consciousness.

Why is all this so important? In the past, sales and marketing activity involved simple tasks that could be performed by one individual, possibly with some help. In comparison, working as a Team to build a *21st Century Financial Practice™* that attracts, services, and retains affluent clients involves a gigantic and complex set of interrelated tasks. Can you imagine a developing Wealth Management Team failing to reach their production goal and still distributing bonuses? That is exactly what happened in the following case.

*Barry, a one-dimensional advisor in Team Building tran-
sition, enlisted the support of his Assistant. When they only
hit five of the six measurements according to his Metrics
Scorecards, although the goal for sales commissions was
missed by 15%, there was still growth. So Barry presented
his Assistant with a $10,000 bonus and a Rolex watch!*

*Now before you gasp too loudly, you should know that one
of his Assistant's Development Goals was to earn her Certified Financial Planner designation. When it took her nearly
18 months, in the midst of hitting all the measurements
except production, she deserved her reward. A good rule-of-
thumb is that as long as the majority of measurements are
reached, everyone who is performing their delegated Areas
of Responsibility and is committed to their areas of development deserves to be recognized and rewarded.*

More than you've ever imagined before, the client loyalty outcome
you seek is totally dependent on how well you all perform and constantly
improve that complex, integrated set of responsibilities. With sales numbers, you could set a quarterly goal and know whether or not you met it.
Not so with client loyalty.

Client loyalty is a goal you will forever pursue, but never allow yourself to believe that it has been achieved. You will periodically measure
it (see Chapter 14), but only to see how far you have progressed. This
means that your recognition and reward system must refocus away from
end results and be directed toward the continuous improvement efforts and
outcomes you all make on a day-to-day basis.

Reward service as well as productivity; including service to each other
(internal service) as well as to clients (external service). Recognize and
reward the behavior you want. Provide incentives and other rewards or
recognition for people who reduce errors, cut costs, increase productivity,

provide excellent service, reduce time wasters, etc. When recognition and/or reward opportunities arise, here are some important guidelines to follow.

- When you *recognize* an individual, don't just say something like, "You're doing a good job." Focus on specific actions they've taken and tell them why you are singling them out for recognition at this time.

- You should also look for tangible ways to *reward* people periodically. A Friday off or a gift certificate doesn't cost much, but each goes a long way in rewarding (and recognizing) achievement. Make certain each reward is tied to a specific activity or series of activities, and explain specifically why they are being rewarded.

When basic needs are being adequately met, you encourage everyone to look ahead and focus on Team goals. This also causes everyone to look inward and think about where they might improve to help the Team achieve those goals. That desire to grow individually so you can grow collectively needs to be tapped.

Establishing Individual Development Goals

Development Goals typically consist of books or articles to read, a course or workshop to attend, a certification standard to achieve, etc. The problem is that these are actually the *means* to achieving a Development Goal – but not the goal itself. Unless all that reading and studying is directed toward a defined end, the effort may contribute little, if anything, to achieving Team goals.

Before determining which courses to take, books to read, etc., you need to identify three contributing factors in goal development.

- The desired Area of Responsibility to be expanded and/or improved *plus* the specific *performance* needed to successfully achieve it.

- The specific *new knowledge* needed to perform that expanded and/or improved responsibility.

- The specific *new skills* needed to perform that expanded and/or improved responsibility.

What do I need to do that I cannot do adequately now? That's the *performance* question. What do I need to know that I don't know now? That's the *knowledge* question. What abilities and skills must I develop to perform at the competency level required? That's the *skill* question. The answers to these questions become your *Individual Development Goals*. With the answers to these questions, you can determine the *means* (e.g., books, articles, classes, workshops, certifications) that will enable the individual to acquire the knowledge and develop the skills.

As you meet with each individual Team Member to identify their *Individual Development Goals*, you will want to evaluate their willingness and ability to do what it takes to accomplish the goals, as well as help them determine a plan of attack toward achieving increased Operational Efficiency, individually and as a Team. Taking these steps will inevitably enable you as a Team to know "where you are going" and will help you to "get there."

Documenting
Operational Efficiency

---

*Common sense is merely genius
disguised in working clothes.*

Thomas Jefferson

My latest visit to our family dentist provided a perfect illustration of a process driven operation that adheres to a documented set of policies and procedures. As I checked in and waited for my name to be called, everything seemed familiar, but there was also a change. A new face greeted me and walked me to the chair for my cleaning. The dental hygienist who had cleaned my teeth for the past 15 years had retired.

Procedurally, everything remained the same. Our conversation was more of getting to know each other, but my teeth and gums went through the workout I remembered all too well. When the dentist appeared to spend five minutes looking into my mouth, checking last visit's x-rays, etc., I encountered another new face, but not really. This new dentist was a former hygienist who had worked in the practice a number of years earlier, and had often cleaned my children's teeth. I had wondered why we hadn't seen her for a while, and now I knew. She had gone to dental school and was now back as a junior partner to her former boss; and will eventually take over his practice when he retires.

Similar to your world, there are distinct regulations governing the dental profession. In this case, there could be no question regarding the competency of either the new hygienist or dentist. It was the way they did things, their "process," that made the experience so familiar. In discussing this with the senior dentist, he attributed it all to having documented policies and procedures and good people who are willing to follow them. He made an important point when he stated, "This is how I keep the confidence of my dental patients when they encounter new people in my practice. The face is new, but the experience remains the same." It sounded so simple.

Imagine a former Assistant serving as a Financial Advisor to one of your key clients. At the same time, you have just brought in a brand new practice manager. Then imagine receiving the ultimate compliment from the client, "I see you have some new people, but I'm pleased to see that I am still receiving the same type and quality of service."

As you walk around any Financial Advisor's office, you'll see shelves filled with documents; many are rarely (if ever) used. Documentation has become more of a status symbol than a useful business tool. One tends to think that the more we have, the more important we must be. Just don't ask us what's in all those binders! That's unfortunate, because continuous improvement of Operational Efficiency is impossible without proper Documentation, the fourth "D" of the *Operational Efficiency Process*. Kaizen consciousness quickly fades, unless it's supported by excellent documentation of your process, which is linked to your long-range business plan.

Documents are typically created in order to support something else. That "something else" is what the quality movement calls *standardization*.

In the context of quality improvement, standardization involves selecting one way of doing an activity and then making certain everyone performs that activity the same way every time. The document you create will explain the steps and standards of each activity that supports your *Operational Efficiency Process*. It will also serve as a handy reference for:

- Guiding someone not familiar with the activity, such as a new Team Member.

- Monitoring the performance of an activity.

- Facilitating a Team discussion of how to improve the performance of the activity.

Without accurate documentation of policies and procedures, these activities cannot be carried out. Consistency will be difficult, especially when new people arrive on the scene. Also, if you haven't documented what you are doing, making improvements is impossible. H. James Harrington emphasizes that standardization is a critical part of the improvement process as follows.

> *Real improvement occurs when everyone is performing an activity in the same way so that the results are predictable. When different people approach the same task in many different ways, the results are difficult to control or improve. Standardization is a key step in the improvement cycle.*

James Harrington would be impressed with how my dentist operates his practice. New faces plus documented policies and procedures equals flawless execution. Your challenge is to do exactly the same thing.

Frankly, this is often a difficult concept to swallow for people who are accustomed to working independently. Standardizing activities isn't foreign; we do that when we start performing routine tasks "out of habit", and the outcome becomes predictable under similar circumstances. It's the importance of documenting the process and defining the circumstances that often eludes us.

As things change, such as new people coming on board, the outcome is less predictable. Documentation is what paves the path for change. New people quickly adapt to the process in place, and the standardization continues. You then adjust your document so it will be current when the next change occurs. Soon, this new activity becomes standardized and routine again. Individually, you may not often need documented policies and procedures. But as a Wealth Management Team, creating the right documentation will become a critical factor in supporting your continuous improvement efforts, in making your Kaizen consciousness a reality.

If you've participated in ISO 9000 or any other quality certification process, you know exactly what this means. The first thing ISO 9000 auditors ask when they walk in the door is, "Show me your documentation manual." This manual must be up-to-date as well as a work in progress. The auditor then takes that manual and checks to see if:

- The documented processes and procedures are simply pieces of paper or are they real documents that are guiding your organization to higher quality and efficiency.

- People in your organization are aware of the documents, understand their purpose, and know how to apply them effectively in their daily work.

That's a far cry from the old days when document manuals were created by managers and technical people who didn't understand how things really got done, which is why so many of them ended up sitting on a shelf, ignored.

Your *Team Documentation Manual* isn't going to end up that way, or at least it shouldn't, for the following reasons:

- The only documents it will contain are those created and used by your Team to guide their thinking and actions.

- Team Members who are committed to both the information and the guidance the documents provide shaped the documents.

- If the documents become outdated or are no longer helpful, the Team is committed to changing them.

Creating Your
Wealth Management Team Documentation Manual

Beginning with your 5-Year Business Plan, you have been introduced to 16 concepts up to this point: seven from your *Business Development Process*, two from your *Financial Advisory Process*, and now seven more from your *Operational Efficiency Process*. In Chapters 13 and 14, you will be introduced to two more for a total of 18. The following is a list of the documents we suggest you create from these concepts to include in your manual.

Your Team Documentation Manual

1. From the *Business Development Process*:
   - 5-Year Business Plan
   - Top 25 Net Profit Contribution Client List
   - *Ideal Client Profile*
   - Yearly Metrics Scorecards
   - Quarterly Metrics Scorecards
   - Weekly Metrics Scorecards
   - Fixed Daily Activities (FDAs)

2. From the *Financial Advisory Process*:
   - Your *Financial Advisory Process*
   - Financial Organizer Document List

3. From the *Operational Efficiency Process*:
   - Business Development / Operational Efficiency Worksheet
   - Operations / Operational Efficiency Worksheet
   - Service / Operational Efficiency Worksheet
   - Administration / Operational Efficiency Worksheet
   - Client Contact Performance Standards
   - *Financial Advisory Process* Performance Standards
   - Individual Development Goals Worksheets for each Team Member

4. From the *Client Loyalty Process*:
   - Strategies for Building Client Loyalty
   - Client Loyalty Profiles

Establishing a
Team Documentation Manual Review Schedule

There are documents that should be reviewed weekly, quarterly, yearly, and whenever someone sees a reason to make a change. Following is a suggested document review schedule.

Team Documentation Manual Review Schedule

1. Weekly:
   - Weekly Metrics Scorecard

2. Quarterly:
   - Quarterly Metrics Scorecard

- Fixed Daily Activities (FDAs)
- Top 25 Net Profit Contribution Client List
- *Ideal Client Profile*
- Your *Financial Advisory Process*
- Financial Organizer Document List
- Strategies for Building Client Loyalty
- Client Loyalty Profiles

3. When someone sees a reason to make a change:
   - Client Contact and *Financial Advisory Process* Performance Standards
   - All four types of Operational Efficiency Worksheets
   - Development Goals Worksheets

4. Yearly:
   - 5-Year Business Plan
   - Yearly Metrics Scorecard

Operational Efficiency is the "grunt work" of establishing and maintaining a competitive edge. There's nothing glamorous about it. Frankly, that's why many Wealth Management Teams will find it increasingly difficult to maintain any advantage they might achieve in the beginning. It requires unfamiliar and often uncomfortable effort. But, it's sure worth it!

We used to believe Operational Efficiency was something to be delegated to others so we would be free to make the decisions and do the "important" stuff. That no longer works; in fact, it never did. Operational Efficiency must be a *total Team effort*. If not, you will quickly revert back to simply assigning tasks and have otherwise competent people standing around waiting for someone to tell them what to do, and not be prepared to handle critical situations on their own. But, a dental clinic in Greensboro,

North Carolina is not going to have anything over a true Wealth Management Team, in terms of clientele, revenue, or Operational Efficiency.

Possessing a manual of basic policies and procedures is common sense and common practice for many businesses. Having a working document that goes one step further and contains your long-range business plan, short-term goals, and a system of measurements that includes every member of the Team is also common sense; but not common practice. In the words of one of our founding fathers, "Common sense is genius disguised in working clothes." Your *Operational Efficiency Process* is what will enable your dreams to put on work clothes and make those dreams come true.

The

Client Loyalty
Process

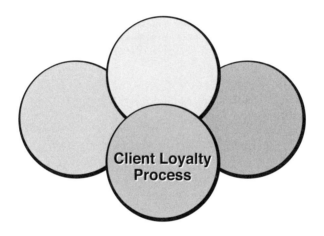

Client Loyalty
Process

Chapter 13
Creating a Client-Oriented Environment

Chapter 14
Making Client Loyalty
Every Team Member's Responsibility

Creating a
Client-Oriented Environment

To business that we love,
we rise betimes,
and go to it with delight.

William Shakespeare

"I couldn't believe it," moaned Gary, a 27-year veteran Financial Advisor working as an independent and considered a top achiever by most industry standards. "Phil's more than a client. He's become a personal friend. I play golf with him, for cryin' out loud! So what does he do? He transfers his account to some Financial Planner with the excuse that he needs more than mutual funds. What a slap in the face!"

Gary was in shock, actually fighting depression. Sure, he isn't going to miss any meals, but his pride was seriously wounded. More important, he couldn't think of any logical reasons for what was happening. This golfing friend was actually his third "key" client to leave over the past three months.

Gary's assessment of all this was based on criteria he has always assumed to be most important. "Haven't I consistently put him in funds that provided good returns (averaged 16% over the past five years)? Beating the S & P, isn't that

---

what it's all about?" Even though these were the thoughts going through his mind, he was beginning to wonder about those assumptions. From his point of view, he had delivered the goods to his golfing buddy, and to the others. They had seemed to be satisfied with those returns. What happened?

A conversation with Carol, his indispensable Assistant of 11 years, began to shed some much needed light on the situation. Carol, also fully licensed, handles most of the correspondence and many of the client phone calls and e-mail messages. "Where's the loyalty?" Gary began. "If I am producing the returns for them, why wouldn't they remain loyal to me?" Focusing on his golfing buddy, the one that puzzled Gary the most, they began to fit the pieces of the puzzle together.

"I suspect it began about a year ago," said Carol. "That's when Phil called and asked for a comprehensive financial plan. Remember? I told you about that, and you said you'd get back to him. I don't think you ever did." "You're right," Phil thoughtfully responded. "My calls and letters to him have mostly been to keep him advised of his returns and growing account. He's mentioned things like retirement funding, college for his two teenage children, and such. I've simply acknowledged them from time to time, suggesting that they will be taken care of if we can just keep the growth rate where it is. He would always tell me he was satisfied with the growth, but I guess that wasn't enough. One thing's for sure - we missed the boat somewhere along the way."

Gary's story is not unique. We've heard it many times, and it's become increasingly familiar over the past five years. The bad news for Gary is that he is losing clients – affluent, influential clients who are the core of his business and his most important source of referrals. As an independent businessman, this can be a scary proposition. The good news is that Gary and Carol are beginning to understand why it's happening. They are coming to grips with the challenges of maintaining Client Loyalty, and that is the all-important first step toward finding a solution.

The Way It *Was*

Merrill Lynch would typically lead the field. They were the largest player, staffed with creative decision makers, and invested heavily in developing products and tools to assist their brokers far into the future. When former CEO Donald Regan decided to challenge banks by creating a Cash Management Account (CMA), their brokers resisted. But Merrill persevered, taught their brokers how to sell this new platform, attached meaningful incentives, and took a distinct lead in developing a distribution channel of financial professionals trained in gathering assets. The term *financial professional* is important here because this represents one of the early efforts to penetrate a market segment (banking services) that, prior to deregulation, had been unavailable. For the individual broker, it was the first baby step toward servicing a broader range of financial needs.

E.F. Hutton, a former boutique wirehouse, was the first to introduce the concept of compensation in the form of a fee on assets rather than the old form of commission per transaction. Merrill Lynch took the lead in getting their brokers to use a basic financial planning tool, *Financial Foundations.* And again, they led the field by developing a distribution force of financial professionals trained in using (and selling) this tool. Today, developments in software have made financial planning tools so commonplace throughout the industry that experts have taken to calling them *McPlans*. The June 2001 issue of *Registered Representative* magazine listed and briefly described 64 such programs from 27 different venders.

A *Consumer Reports* article titled "Financial Fixers and Fakers" (January, 1998) outlined the realities facing financial professionals and investors in the 21st century. The article title actually speaks for itself. Of the 500,000 people marketing financial products and services, less than 7% had earned a Certified Financial Planner designation at that point. Less than 1% were paid based on the services they provide, rather than on the commissions generated from the financial products they recommended (sold). After stating these important facts, the article proceeded to analyze each plan. You can read the findings at your local library if you're interested, but they were not flattering. And that raises a key question: Are Affluent Investors ignorant of all this? Answer: Not hardly!

The Way It *Is*

As we entered the 21st century, individual financial professionals and their companies were slowly beginning to reposition themselves to meet the needs of the Affluent Investor; recognizing that they want an unbiased financial professional who understands the finer nuances of financial planning, who will provide timely advice and will also make everything clear. One of the key concepts that surfaced continually throughout our research is that Affluent Investors will pay for value, for investment knowledge and extraordinary service.

In effect, many of the services provided by stockbrokers, insurance companies, and banks are becoming commoditized through technology. As a result, potential clients are better informed, financial services companies are converging their markets, and financial professionals are being held to a higher standard than ever before. This is especially true with Affluent Investors who, because of the incredible growth of this market segment, have become the prized target for everyone everywhere. Many financial services firms are making the effort to shift from their traditional transactional business to financial planning platforms, often in the form of fee-based compensation. Yet, something seems to be missing. Are they – are you – truly prepared to meet the demands and desires of Affluent Investors? Do you know how to gain and retain their loyalty?

Gary thought he accomplished this by breaking away from his parent company, a large insurance firm, to establish a practice that allowed him to get more involved with investments. His investment product of choice became a handful of mutual fund families. Up until a couple of years ago he had no doubts about his decision to go it alone. He was able to make decisions regarding both his practice and his clients without all the red tape of a large firm and, as a result, was able to create a very lucrative practice. He looked after his clients and socialized with them. Until recently, they were extremely loyal. But the needs, wants, and expectations of Affluent Investors are changing, as Gary now realizes.

The Search For A Loyal Client

Telephone books are filled with business names that employ the words *quick, jiffy, instant, one-hour, quality*, and so on. People may take months to shoot a roll of film, but when they take that last shot, they become very impatient about getting their pictures back. If you accepted the claims of all those advertisements, you'd assume that every company in the land puts the customer first. But you know they don't – and you also know that you must.

You have been preparing to offer a wide range of services and advice to meet the multidimensional financial needs of Affluent Investors. Not only that, but everything you have done to this point focuses on providing Ritz Carlton level service with FedEx efficiency. There is one critical element left.

If you have clients in the upper-middle class or affluent category, you have probably worked hard to build a personal relationship with them. That only makes good sense, or so you think. You would be amazed at how many financial professionals who, like Gary, have told us about high net worth clients that they suddenly lost to a competitor. In almost every case, the cry of frustration was, "I thought we were friends. He was even my golf buddy, for cryin' out loud!"

That statement goes to the heart of the issue. Good friends and golf buddies do not necessarily make *loyal* clients if all you have established with them is a personal relationship. That relationship may have delayed the breakup a bit, but it won't prevent it from ultimately happening. A *loyal* client happens as the result of a highly valued, ongoing *professional* relationship.

Professional relationships build on how effectively "what you do for them" meets and exceeds their expectations. Being satisfied today with what you did for them today isn't enough. But if you are successful in building the kind of professional relationship that earns your client's *loyalty*, you will know it because in return, they will do the following:

- In addition to conducting business with you today, they will indicate their willingness to continue doing business with *only you* in the future.

- They will eagerly consider new strategies, services, and products that you recommend and can effectively link to their financial needs.

- They will resist the "pull" from your competition, and you will know they did because they will tell you they did.

- They will provide introductions and referrals when asked; and may even provide unsolicited referrals without being asked.

You build Client Loyalty through everything you've learned up to this point. That's foundational, but there is more. You must build on that foundation by deliberately and systematically doing these three things:

- Work with your Team to create a client-oriented environment; an office environment that is convenient for your clients, not just for you.

- Make Client Loyalty the *primary* responsibility of every Team Member. This isn't just a banner to hang on the wall. There are specific elements required to make this a reality.

- Equip and prepare yourselves for the key interaction points you typically have with clients.

Creating a Client-Oriented Environment

The recommendations that follow do not include everything you can do, but they do cover key strategies that you should do in order to create a "client friendly" office environment. As you review these strategies, note that many will enable you to effectively address the unique needs and desires of each client.

1. Create a respectful business atmosphere, especially if clients frequently come to your office for the services you provide. Don't try to impress clients. Create a comfortable office environment that is consistent with their lifestyle. Remember that many upper-middle class and affluent clients came from modest backgrounds and have a commitment to that lifestyle. If your office environment looks too "rich," they may be concerned that you are getting rich off of them.

   Practice hospitality by doing the little things. Be there to greet clients when they come in the door. You, not an Assistant! Don't make them sit in front of a receptionist waiting until you get off the phone. Hold doors open for people. When you are finished, walk them to the elevator, to the lobby, or even to their car.

Make certain that restrooms, coffee rooms, etc. are spotless – all the time.

Don't tell people about your service. Show them.

2. Be available to clients 24 hours a day, even if you don't believe that it's necessary. Get rid of the "9 to 5, Monday through Friday" restrictive feeling that businesses typically project, especially those in financial services. On your literature, state something like "our office hours are whatever you need them to be."

One call should be all that is required for a client to contact you. Hire an answering service, with clear instructions regarding the person on the Team that should be contacted. You can (and should) distribute the responsibility to be "on-call" among your Team Members. Someone should be able to respond to a client call within 15 minutes, regardless of when it is received.

3. This one builds on Number 1. When a client asks any Team Member "Can you...?", the only answer you will give is "Yes", even if you can't immediately figure out how to do what they want.

Be prepared to find *anything* they want, regardless of what it is. Don't charge for this "extra" service unless absolutely necessary. If you must charge, discuss it with them ahead of time once you have determined what the cost will be. Will they take advantage of you? Rarely, if ever.

4. Enable clients to help you provide Ritz-Carlton level service, by communicating the following information.

- Explain your overall *Financial Advisory Process* in the beginning and then explain each step again before you launch into it. When you go over each step, cover the following five points:

  1) This is *what* we will be doing.

  2) These are the *results* you can expect.

  3) This is what *we* will do to make this step successful.

  4) This is what we need *you* to do to make this step successful.

  5) This is the *benefit* you will receive from this step.

- Tell them the *best time* to contact you. "You can contact us any time day or night, but the best times are between _____ and _____ on _____."

- When they request help for something, tell them exactly what *information they need to provide* in order for you to help them in this specific area.

5. Become a leadership example. Don't expect Team Members to exhibit desired attitudes and behavior unless they *first* see them in you. They will tend to do what you do, and they will justify it on that basis.

Making Client Loyalty
The Primary Responsibility of Every Team Member

The first step is to tell your Team that everyone is responsible for building Client Loyalty and explain why. The next step is to initiate Team activities that will encourage that responsibility. Here are three activities that will help you do that:

1. Challenge every Team Member to become obsessed with knowing everything they can about every client. In 1988, Harvey MacKay wrote a book titled *Swim with the Sharks* where he presented strategies for "outselling, outmanaging, outmotivating, and outnegotiating your competition." One strategy was centered on knowing everything possible about your customer and his 66-Question Customer Profile became the most talked-about part of his book. Sixty-six questions might be stretching it a bit, but the principle is sound, so you can start with the following:

   - Set up a *client database* that everyone can access any time.

   - Challenge everyone to gather information and enter it into the database. Explain that even if they pick up information that is already posted on the database, the constant probing is the real value of this activity.

   - Set up a system whereby anyone who is in contact with a client can easily access that client's database – before the contact if possible.

   - Review the client databases at Team meetings and use them to guide your day-to-day feedback (above) and "Keep In Touch" meetings and events (see the next section).

2. Keep a Mistake Log System, asking every Team Member to log every mistake made. This will only be possible when you create an atmosphere where correcting mistakes (reducing waste) is very important and *placing blame is not permitted*. Following is a suggested format.

   - Date

   - Client Involved

- What Happened

- How It Was Resolved

- Final Results

Have each Team Member present his or her latest mistake. Use the following questions to process them.

- What happened?

- What was done to satisfy the customer? (congratulate them)

- What caused the mistake?

- What will be done to prevent that mistake from recurring?

Brainstorm together for answers to the last question, but allow the individual to select the solution they will use. Make reviewing the Mistake Logs a regular agenda item at Team meetings so you can constantly look for ways to improve.

3. Constantly search for new ideas. Set up a New Ideas Log System, encouraging all Team Members to place ideas on the log for discussion at your next Team meeting. A suggested format follows.

- Date

- Idea

- Area of Responsibility

- Team Member(s) Submitting

To enhance the Team's interaction on ideas, set up an on-line Message Board (also called a Discussion Forum). Encourage Team Members to post ideas and notify other Team Members, so that they can provide feedback and interact with each other about the ideas. Here are a couple of sources.

- Inside The Web   *http://www.insidetheweb.com*

- YourBBS.com   *http://www.yourbbs.com*

Select some aspect of your Business Development, Operations, Service, or Administrative Areas of Responsibility where you are not as efficient as you would like. Ask Team Members to help find another organization that performs in that area exceptionally well. Contact that organization and ask if you could visit them to "benchmark" what they do. If they agree, have the Team Member in the Lead Role visit and document what they do. In fact, other Team Members involved in that area could also go. They should then report back to the Team, and together you should agree on what will be done to improve.

Interacting With Each Client at Appropriate Points

We all understand the value of interacting with clients. The key in building Client Loyalty with affluent clients is to interact with them at "appropriate" points.

Appropriate interaction occurs when it provides valued benefit to both the client and to you. Too often, we set up meetings or social events to meet our own objectives without considering how it will benefit the client. We will be looking at the following three types of appropriate interaction points:

- Day-To-Day Communication

- Keep-In-Touch Meetings and Social Events

- Creative Recovery

1. **Day-To-Day Communication**. You obviously don't communicate with every client every day, but there should be a daily effort to find appropriate reasons to communicate with one or more clients. Here are some tips.

   - Handwritten notes are often the best.

   - As you get to know more about each client, you will be able to acknowledge something in their personal or business life as well as express appreciation for having them as a client.

   - Send birthday, anniversary, graduation, etc., cards to everyone in the family, not just to the client.

   - Personally attend important family events, especially those appropriate to the business relationship you have with the client. For example, assume you are involved with a client in education planning for a son who is just entering his senior year of high school. It would be very appropriate to attend his graduation plus other senior year activities that are very important to him and his parents.

   - If you use a newsletter, consider setting aside one section (up to ½ page) to personalize for each client. You can use that section for a personal update.

2. **Keep-In-Touch Meetings and Social Events**. "Appropriate" is especially important here, because upper-middle class and affluent clients are not eager to simply attend meetings and events. Those meetings and events must add value to their relationship with you. Every meeting and event must be selected and planned with client benefit in mind. They must believe they will benefit from participating. Here are some ideas.

- Create a "client benefit statement" for each meeting and event you plan. Incorporate it into your invitation. *Never* invite a client to a meeting or event with a "hidden agenda" that they will only discover after they arrive.

- Invite select individual clients to come and speak to your Team about some aspect of their world that impacts your *Financial Advisory Process* and the services you provide. People love talking about themselves, and the client involved will be impressed with your efforts to understand them better. Also, this provides an opportunity for your entire Team to interact with a client – which enhances their understanding and helps cement their relationship with that client.

- Follow up with a "thank you" detailing what you learned and how you plan to use it.

- Update meetings should only be used when face-to-face communication is important – such as when you need to show them information, explain it, and use it to make on-the-spot decisions. Otherwise use phone, e-mail or fax.

- Every social event communicates a message. Inviting clients to a symphony is quite different from inviting them to a baseball game; both in terms of the conversation that takes place during the event and where you go and what you do afterwards. The more you are in tune with their interests, the greater value the event will be to them. You will also benefit from spending a relaxing time with them in their world.

3. **Creative Recovery**. Encourage clients to complain, and make it easy for them to do so. Encourage them to contact you if something is not right, and provide them with an easy way to do that – a phone number

that is always answered, an e-mail address that you check at least three times a day, etc.

Train your Team Members to handle complaints effectively. There should be a local organization that provides customer service training. Have them come in and work with your Team; and make certain they use lots of role-play so you can practice!

Complaints should be dealt with promptly and "managed" by the Team Member who makes the contact (see the client interaction performance standards defined in Chapter 9). The basic process for handling complaints is presented below.

Handling Client Complaints

What clients want, when they complain, is respect, an apology and a solution. Follow these steps:

1. Restate the complaint and apologize with empathy.

2. Fix it as quickly and efficiently as possible.

3. Do something extra to show you care.

4. Follow up to make certain your solution was successful.

What's so new about these strategies? Nothing, as a matter of fact! But if you're not using them, they are new to you, and they need to be used. This is Kaizen consciousness in action. These strategies will help you to make continuous improvement a reality, and the outcome will be a level of Client Loyalty unmatched. Gary had been following most of the strategies, but not all. His biggest mistake was not listening to the marketplace. Remember, times are changin', and fast!

Measuring
Client Loyalty

The person who renders loyal service
in a humble capacity will be
chosen for higher responsibilities...

B. C. Forbes

In Chapter 5, you were introduced to the concept of a metrics system as a way of linking ongoing performance to factors that are true indicators of future success. You learned how weekly, quarterly, and yearly Metrics Scorecards could help you track those factors and then make adjustments to your efforts so you could ultimately produce the results you want.

In this chapter, we cover another measurement method for you to use in monitoring the most important of all the results you seek – *Client Loyalty*. This measurement method comes in the form of a *profile*. A profile is like a snapshot. It enables you to see something as it exists right now – frozen in time. It permits you to examine it carefully and think about what you can do to make it better in the future.

I actually know of a major wealth management trust company that is beginning to lose clients to a select group of new competitors. This has never happened before. What is most amazing to this particular trust company is that these new competitors are two small Wealth Management Teams, Financial Advisors just like you, who have invested the time, energy, and resources into making the transition from the sales and marketing model of Wall Street to creating a true *21st Century Financial Practice™*. Granted, they are initially picking off the low hanging fruit from this trust company, but it is fruit that has never been picked before, plucked from a company that has been resting too long on its laurels.

These new competitors are hungry, aggressive, solutions-based, and process driven. They are providing everything this long-standing wealth management institution provides, but even more. Because they are able to deliver hands-on service, solve ongoing problems, provide sound investment advice, and personally manage the relationship (all for a reasonable fee); Client Loyalty is becoming a reality and word-of-mouth influence is emerging as the focal point of their business development efforts.

Once you have developed the three other processes (*Business Development, Financial Advisory,* and *Operational Efficiency*) you are ready for the most enjoyable, and arguably the process with the most long-term significance – the *Client Loyalty Process*.

After formulating a strategy for building Client Loyalty, you will need a way to measure the results of that effort. In a nutshell, that is the purpose behind the *Ideal Client Profile*.

Earlier we distinguished between a *satisfied* and a *loyal* client by looking at what they *do* differently. Research shows clearly that being satisfied with a given transaction is not enough. Satisfied clients frequently leave; loyal clients have stick-ability. Since what your clients do is the outcome of what you do, it makes perfect sense to use those Client Loyalty behaviors as the basis for measuring the impact of what you have been doing. Here is what you can expect a Loyal Client to do:

- Conduct business with you now.

- Conduct business with *only* you in the future.

- Eagerly consider new strategies, services, products, etc. that you recommend.

- Resist the "pull" from your competition.

- Provide solicited and unsolicited introductions and referrals.

For *each* client who either matches your *Ideal Client Profile* or is in the process of being upgraded to that level, you should:

- Complete the *Client Loyalty Profile* (shown on the following two pages) about six months after you have placed them on your Ideal Client or upgrade list.

- Review and update each *Client Loyalty Profile* every six months thereafter.

As you will note, the *Client Loyalty Profile* is a composite of key items from your *Business Development* and *Financial Advisory Processes*, plus your efforts to establish a client-oriented environment. You may have other items you feel should be added as well.

It is highly unlikely that the trust company described earlier in this chapter is applying anything like this to their smaller clients. If they were, our recently formed Wealth Management Teams would be encountering much more difficulty in prying away any clientele with less than $20 million in assets. Think of this as your sweet spot. Those Affluent Investors with between 1 and 20 million dollars need solutions for the multidimensional aspects of their finances; they want a plan they can follow and understand; and they expect Ritz-Carlton service delivered with FedEx efficiency. They also want a relationship manager who cares!

Remember the prominent wirehouse that lost as many $1 million accounts as it took in during 2000? I would wager that most of those brokers who lost $1 million accounts did not have any of these processes at work, much less a method for measuring Client Loyalty.

Client Loyalty Profile

Client Name: _____ Date:_____

Assets Under Management:

We currently manage _____% of their total assets.

The other _____% is managed by:_____

Solutions Offered and Used:

Solution	Date Offered	Used (Yes/No)
Budgeting, Cash Flow Mgmt, Determining Net Worth.	_____	_____
Insurance Planning	_____	_____
Investment Administration	_____	_____
Education Planning	_____	_____
Tax Planning	_____	_____
Retirement Planning	_____	_____
Estate Planning	_____	_____
Charitable Giving	_____	_____

Reasons given for not accepting your offers to include solutions:

_____

_____

Changes in Client Loyalty status over past 6 months:

How many times have you learned about offers from competitors that the client rejected? _____

Details: _____

How many unsolicited introductions or referrals have they provided you? _____

Details: _____

What was their response when you asked for introductions or referrals?

Details: _____

Have you received any complaints about the fees they pay you and/or the fee structure you use?

Details: _____

List below the specific interactions you have had at appropriate points with this client over the past 6 months:

Day-To-Day Communication

_____

_____

Keep-In-Touch Meetings and Social Events

_____

_____

Creative Recovery

_____

_____

Other comments about your efforts to gain and maintain this client's loyalty:

_____

_____

On a scale of 10 (high) to 1 (low), your Team assesses this client as being at a level _____ in terms of Client Loyalty. Your reasons are:

_____

_____

_____

The key to your *Client Loyalty Process* is to create and carefully examine that "snapshot in time" with an eye toward the future. The vital message that comes from your effort here is that your future is now! You look at the present, to evaluate what you did in the past, so you can improve in the future. Once again, we find Kaizen consciousness in action.

Your Future Is Now

Chapter 15
Benchmarking Your Future

Chapter 16
Preparing Today for Tomorrow's Opportunities

Benchmarking
Your Future

Never take anything for granted.
Benjamin Disraeli

I was sitting on the beach with my brother, part of our annual family vacation ritual, and after thoroughly exhausting the topic of sports, our conversation turned to business. I know, it shouldn't happen on vacation; but I had a good reason. Paul is the CFO of a Fortune 100 company and, with his sharp mind, has a knack for cutting right to the chase and simplifying a complex subject. I pick up some great insights from him.

Our conversation somehow got around to benchmarking. He explained what a valuable process it has become for their company. "Actually," he said, "it's simpler than a lot of people realize. We consistently benchmark what we do against the best practices in our industry. Then we initiate a process to quickly close whatever *gaps* we uncover. It keeps us on the cutting edge." As I described how we pulled criteria out of our research and developed a *benchmarking tool* that is being used by financial professionals looking to develop Wealth Management Teams, he gave a typical Paul-type response, "That's good, they should!"

Benchmarking is a technique used by successful companies in all sectors of business. It has proved to be a streamlined and highly effective tool for helping organizations become as good as the best in areas that are critical to their success. By comparing what you do with those who do it much better, you can clearly define *performance gaps* that need priority attention. In this chapter, you will have an opportunity to compare your current financial practice against 25 benchmarking criteria that we drew from the research that shaped the four phases of our *21st Century Financial Practice™* model.

Although we believe that what we have presented here represents the *best of the best* for a Team approach to attract, service, and retain Affluent Investor clients; we cannot impose that opinion on you. Therefore, before you compare your present performance against these criteria, you will have an opportunity to determine exactly how important you believe those factors will be to your future success. Our desire is to help you focus your efforts on improving those areas that you believe are most important.

Our *Benchmarking Your Future* self-assessment tool is presented here in its complete form. There are a total of 50 questions. Each question has *seven* possible responses. You are asked to select one response for each question.

Your answers are not a reflection of you personally, but simply a way for you to evaluate how you currently think about and do your financial practice using 25 criteria as a benchmark of comparison. To truly benefit from this exercise, it's important that you answer all questions in terms of *what you actually think and/or do* and not what you believe is the "right answer." This is not a "right answer" test!

Importance Level – 25 questions

Each statement below expresses the *importance* of some aspect of making a financial practice effective. You are to decide how important you believe each statement to be. Then write down the number that best represents your decision using the following scale.

7 – Extremely Important   **3 – Somewhat Important**

6 – Very Important   **2 – Not Very Important**

5 – Quite Important   **1 – Not At All Important**

4 – Moderately Important

How *important* is it for you to:

1. ____ Quit trying to live from transaction-to-transaction and find an effective way to build long-term financial advisory relationships with the clients you want to serve.

2. ____ Focus your business development efforts where the real growth is, toward upper-middle class and affluent investors.

3. ____ Clearly envision your future and create the long-range business plan that you really want to (and believe you can) achieve.

4. ____ Use a system that keeps you focused on the strategies and tactics that will really make you successful.

5. ____ Gather vital information about upper-middle class and affluent market segments, and use that information to define your future ideal client.

6. ____ Abandon the old prospect attraction methods that aren't working, find out what really does work with upper-middle class and affluent clients, and learn how to use those tactics successfully.

7. ____ Project the right image to upper-middle class and affluent people.

8. ____ Use a promotional piece that goes beyond stating what you do and clearly communicates the benefits of working with you.

9. ____ Connect quickly and effectively when talking with upper-middle class and affluent people.

10.____ Qualify and close the prospects you want to work with – those who are from upper-middle class and affluent market segments.

11.____ Expand your expertise so you can offer solutions to the multi-dimensional financial needs of upper-middle class and affluent clients.

12.____ Create a step-by-step *Financial Advisory Process* that enables you to cover the basics plus adapt it to the unique needs of each client.

13.____ Interview clients in a way that educates them and gets them to provide critical information while earning their trust.

14.____ Provide each client with a Financial Organizer that enables them to organize and easily access the information and documents they receive throughout each step of your *Financial Advisory Process.*

15.____ Have a Wealth Management Team in place that matches Ritz-Carlton quality of service and FedEx efficiency, even if it only involves yourself and a shared assistant.

16.____ Coordinate everything with a focus toward providing value-added service for your clients.

7–Extremely 6–Very 5–Quite 4–Moderately 3–Somewhat 2–Not Very 1–Not At All

17.____ Enable Team Members to establish and achieve professional development goals that are tied to improving specific areas of responsibility.

18.____ Conduct highly effective Team meetings.

19.____ Create a manual containing goals, policies, procedures, and responsibilities that doesn't just sit on a shelf, but is used continually to guide Team efforts.

20.____ Build long-term client loyalty as opposed to simply trying to satisfy clients with each transaction.

21.____ Use client loyalty as your essential competitive edge strategy.

22.____ Make client loyalty the primary responsibility of each Team Member, and together build a client-oriented environment.

23.____ Improve client impact through day-to-day communication, keep-in-touch meetings, social events, and other strategies.

24.____ Creatively recover from client complaints and use those complaints to actually build client loyalty.

25.____ Know exactly where you are and what you need to do to gain and maintain the loyalty of each and every client.

Performance Level – 25 Questions

Each statement below describes the effective *performance* of some aspect of making your financial practice effective. You are to decide how *well* you perform each item as stated. Then write down the number that best represents your decision, using the following scale.

7–Extremely 6–Very 5–Quite 4–Moderately 3–Somewhat 2–Not Very 1–Not At All

7 – Extremely Well   **3 – Somewhat Well**

6 – Very Well   **2 – Not Very Well**

5 – Quite Well   **1 – Not At All Well**

4 – Moderately Well

How *well* are you *performing* in your efforts to:

26.____ Build long-term financial advisory relationships with the clients you want to serve, so that you no longer are trying to live from transaction-to-transaction.

27.____ Keep your business development efforts focused toward upper-middle class and affluent investors – where the real growth is.

28.____ Follow the long-range business plan that you really want – and are demonstrating that you can achieve.

29.____ Follow a system that keeps you focused on strategies and tactics that are really making you successful.

30.____ Use the vital information that you gathered about upper-middle class and affluent market segments to define your future ideal client.

31.____ Use marketing tactics that are highly successful in attracting upper-middle class and affluent clients.

32.____ Always project the right image when networking with upper-middle class and affluent people.

33.____ Use your promotional piece when meeting with upper-middle class and affluent prospects to clearly communicate the benefits of working with you.

34.____ Identify financial impact points and use them to connect quickly and effectively when talking with upper-middle class and affluent people.

35.____ Qualify and close upper-middle class and affluent prospects from the market segment niches you have targeted.

36.____ Offer well-received solutions for all the multidimensional financial needs of upper-middle class and affluent clients.

37.____ Use your step-by-step *Financial Advisory Process* to both cover the basics and adapt to the unique needs of each client.

38.____ Interview clients in a way that educates them while they provide critical information and you earn their trust.

39.____ Use a Financial Organizer for each client that enables them to organize and easily access the information and documents they receive throughout each step of your *Financial Advisory Process.*

40.____ Work so well as a Wealth Management Team that you are able to match Ritz-Carlton quality of service and FedEx efficiency

41.____ Coordinate everything so well that you see clear evidence of providing value-added service for your clients.

42.____ Improve specific areas of responsibility through your efforts to establish and achieve development goals.

43.____ Conduct highly effective Team meetings.

44.____ Use your manual of goals, policies, procedures, and responsibilities to continually guide Team efforts.

7–Extremely 6–Very 5–Quite 4–Moderately 3–Somewhat 2–Not Very 1–Not At All

45.____ Build long-term client loyalty rather than simply trying to satisfy clients with each transaction.

46.____ Use client loyalty as your essential competitive edge strategy.

47.____ Make client loyalty the primary responsibility of each Team Member, and together build a client-oriented environment.

48.____ Improve client impact through day-to-day communication, keep-in-touch meetings, social events, and other strategies.

49.____ Creatively recover from client complaints and use those complaints to actually build client loyalty.

50.____ Create a client profile that records exactly where you are and what you need to do to gain and maintain the loyalty of each and every client.

Next, you have an opportunity to build on your responses to the above 50 questions by:

- Identifying the *performance gaps* between what you are doing and what you judged as important.

- Summarizing your improvement focus for each phase of development.

Identifying Performance Gaps

You identify *Performance Gaps* by calculating the gap that exists between what you judged to be important and what you evaluated your present performance to be.

7–Extremely 6–Very 5–Quite 4–Moderately 3–Somewhat 2–Not Very 1–Not At All

- For each of the 25 benchmarking criteria listed below, transfer the scores you wrote down for the *Importance* and *Performance* questions. The questions are identified by the letters and numbers listed under the blank lines (e.g. Q26 means question #26).

- Then *subtract* the *second score* from the *first score* to determine your *gap* score.

Performance **Score – *Importance* Score = Performance *Gap***

Business Development Process

1. Building long-term financial advisory relationships with the clients you want to serve so that you no longer are trying to live from transaction-to-transaction.

$$\overline{\text{Q26}} - \overline{\text{Q1}} = \overline{\text{Gap}}$$

2. Keeping your business development efforts focused toward upper-middle class and affluent investors – where the real growth is.

$$\overline{\text{Q27}} - \overline{\text{Q2}} = \overline{\text{Gap}}$$

3. Following the long-range business plan that you really want – and are demonstrating that you can achieve.

$$\overline{\text{Q28}} - \overline{\text{Q3}} = \overline{\text{Gap}}$$

4. Following a system that keeps you focused on strategies and tactics that are really making you successful.

$$\overline{\text{Q29}} - \overline{\text{Q4}} = \overline{\text{Gap}}$$

5. Using the vital information that you gathered about upper-middle class and affluent market segments to define your future ideal client.

$$\overline{\text{Q30}} - \overline{\text{Q5}} = \overline{\text{Gap}}$$

6. Using marketing tactics that are highly successful in attracting upper-middle class and affluent clients.

$$\underline{}_{\text{Q31}} - \underline{}_{\text{Q6}} = \underline{}_{\text{Gap}}$$

7. Always projecting the right image when networking with upper-middle class and affluent people.

$$\underline{}_{\text{Q32}} - \underline{}_{\text{Q7}} = \underline{}_{\text{Gap}}$$

8. Using your promotional piece when meeting with upper-middle class and affluent prospects to clearly communicate the benefits of working with you.

$$\underline{}_{\text{Q33}} - \underline{}_{\text{Q8}} = \underline{}_{\text{Gap}}$$

9. Identifying financial impact points and using them to connect quickly and effectively when talking with upper-middle class and affluent people.

$$\underline{}_{\text{Q34}} - \underline{}_{\text{Q9}} = \underline{}_{\text{Gap}}$$

10. Qualifying and closing upper-middle class and affluent prospects from the market segment niches you have targeted.

$$\underline{}_{\text{Q35}} - \underline{}_{\text{Q10}} = \underline{}_{\text{Gap}}$$

Financial Advisory Process

11. Offering well-received solutions for all the multidimensional financial needs of upper-middle class and affluent clients.

$$\underline{}_{\text{Q36}} - \underline{}_{\text{Q11}} = \underline{}_{\text{Gap}}$$

12. Using your step-by-step *Financial Advisory Process* to both cover the basics and adapt to the unique needs of each client.

$$\underline{}_{\text{Q37}} - \underline{}_{\text{Q12}} = \underline{}_{\text{Gap}}$$

13. Interviewing clients in a way that educates them while they provide critical information and you earn their trust.

$$\underline{\quad}_{\textbf{Q38}} - \underline{\quad}_{\textbf{Q13}} = \underline{\quad}_{\textbf{Gap}}$$

14. Using a Financial Organizer for each client that enables them to organize and easily access the information and documents they receive throughout each step of your *Financial Advisory Process.*

$$\underline{\quad}_{\textbf{Q39}} - \underline{\quad}_{\textbf{Q14}} = \underline{\quad}_{\textbf{Gap}}$$

Operational Efficiency Process

15. Working so well as a Wealth Management Team that you are able to match Ritz-Carlton quality of service and FedEx efficiency.

$$\underline{\quad}_{\textbf{Q40}} - \underline{\quad}_{\textbf{Q15}} = \underline{\quad}_{\textbf{Gap}}$$

16. Coordinating everything so well that you see clear evidence of providing value-added service for your clients.

$$\underline{\quad}_{\textbf{Q41}} - \underline{\quad}_{\textbf{Q16}} = \underline{\quad}_{\textbf{Gap}}$$

17. Improving efficiency in particular areas of responsibility through your efforts to establish and achieve development goals.

$$\underline{\quad}_{\textbf{Q42}} - \underline{\quad}_{\textbf{Q17}} = \underline{\quad}_{\textbf{Gap}}$$

18. Conducting highly effective Team meetings.

$$\underline{\quad}_{\textbf{Q43}} - \underline{\quad}_{\textbf{Q18}} = \underline{\quad}_{\textbf{Gap}}$$

19. Using your manual of goals, policies, procedures, and responsibilities to continually guide Team efforts.

$$\underline{\quad}_{\textbf{Q44}} - \underline{\quad}_{\textbf{Q19}} = \underline{\quad}_{\textbf{Gap}}$$

Client Loyalty Process

20. Building long-term client loyalty rather than simply trying to satisfy clients with each transaction.

$$\underline{\hspace{1cm}} - \underline{\hspace{1cm}} = \underline{\hspace{1cm}}$$
Q45 **Q20** **Gap**

21. Using client loyalty as your essential competitive edge strategy.

$$\underline{\hspace{1cm}} - \underline{\hspace{1cm}} = \underline{\hspace{1cm}}$$
Q46 **Q21** **Gap**

22. Making client loyalty the primary responsibility of each Team Member, and together building a client-oriented environment.

$$\underline{\hspace{1cm}} - \underline{\hspace{1cm}} = \underline{\hspace{1cm}}$$
Q47 **Q22** **Gap**

23. Improving client impact through day-to-day communication, social events, keep-in-touch meetings, and other strategies.

$$\underline{\hspace{1cm}} - \underline{\hspace{1cm}} = \underline{\hspace{1cm}}$$
Q48 **Q23** **Gap**

24. Creatively recovering from client complaints and using those complaints to actually build client loyalty.

$$\underline{\hspace{1cm}} - \underline{\hspace{1cm}} = \underline{\hspace{1cm}}$$
Q49 **Q24** **Gap**

25. Creating a client loyalty profile that records exactly where you are and what you need to do to gain and maintain the loyalty of each and every client.

$$\underline{\hspace{1cm}} - \underline{\hspace{1cm}} = \underline{\hspace{1cm}}$$
Q50 **Q25** **Gap**

Focusing Improvement Efforts

Next, you will want to analyze any *performance gaps* identified above. Three steps are involved.

1. First you will want to interpret the results.

- By subtracting your *Importance Scores* from your *Performance Scores*, you calculated what we call your Performance Gap Score.

- *Performance gaps* exist when you have a negative gap score. Those scores can range from a -6 (largest gap) to a -1 (smallest gap).

- Gap Scores from 0 to +6 indicate that *no gap exists*, that your performance is equal to or better than the importance you assigned to that item.

2. Next, review the benchmarking criteria, which are described under each of the four processes listed under the *Identifying Performance Gaps* heading. Within each process, identify key areas where you believe development is needed. Use the following guidelines to help you think that through.

   - Identify your *highest* Performance Gap scores. Remember that minus 6 is highest and minus 1 is lowest.

   - Look at the *Importance* score for each of the *gaps* you identified. Items with the higher *Importance* scores are a good place to begin.

   - Read the *descriptive statements* for those criteria you are considering. Then use your gap scores, *Importance* scores, and your own insights to determine where you need to focus your attention

   - List four headings on a piece of paper: *Business Development Process, Financial Advisory Process, Operational Efficiency Process*, and *Client Loyalty Process.* Under each heading, note the specific gaps that you feel need priority attention – and your thoughts on why.

3. Finally, after considering all the *performance gaps* in all four processes, identify the primary *reasons* why you believe those *gaps* exist. Consider the following possibilities:

- I have not spent enough *time* on these areas.

- I lack the *know-how* to perform with excellence in these areas.

- I lack the *skills* to perform with excellence in these areas.

- I do not have *adequate resources* to find good ideas for performing better in these areas.

- Any other reasons and insights that come to mind.

If you're feeling a bit squeamish, relax. I have a vivid recollection of a group of 15 Financial Advisors, senior members of existing Wealth Management Teams, sighing with an air of arrogance as I asked them to take 45 minutes to thoughtfully complete this benchmarking tool. As many workshops as I have conducted, I'm still never quite certain what it will take for participants to put an end to the posturing and begin a sincere commitment to growth and development. With this particular group, I couldn't tell who was posturing and who was simply uncomfortable.

It didn't take long to see that this group of high achievers was basically uncomfortable. The mumbling ranged from "Are you trying to make me feel bad?" to a chorus of "I've got gaps everywhere!" All I could say was, "Thank you benchmarking!" It was only after completing this bench-

marking tool that, despite their past success, this group was ready to embrace the concept of Kaizen. This simple tool served as the foundation upon which they began to build their own 21st Century Financial Practice™.

Every organized effort to achieve anything has gaps. By completing this *benchmarking tool*, you should now have a much clearer picture of the gaps that exist between where you are now and where you want to be; and you have identified key reasons why you believe those gaps exist. The first 14 chapters explained how to do it, so now you are ready to close those gaps and create the *21st Century Financial Practice™* of your dreams.

Preparing Today For Tomorrow's Opportunities

When you come to a fork in the road,
take it.

Yogi Berra

In his terrific book, *Management Challenges for the 21st Century*, Peter Drucker examines the current exploding Information Revolution within the context of three previous Information Revolutions. You will have to read the book to get the full benefit of all the lessons from this great professor, but I'll share one small peril with you.

He asked the rhetorical question, "Is there anything we can learn today, from what happened five hundred years ago?" The third Information Revolution is "what happened," initiated by two inventions between 1450 and 1455 A.D., Gutenberg's printing press and movable type. His answer is quite revealing. "The first thing to learn," Drucker suggests, "is humility."

That makes very good sense. Learning and growing must begin and end with humility. Only in humility can we put aside our pride and arrogance and begin the learning process. Then, as we gain more and more knowledge, we recognize how much we still don't know – especially in this current age of exploding information! That truly does keep us humble.

Humility reminds us that we don't have all the answers and confirms that success is never guaranteed. That's the attitude you must have to truly capitalize on this 21st century model for developing or fine-tuning your Wealth Management Team. The ideas, strategies, and tactics presented in this book offer you an *opportunity*; which according to Webster means you now have within your grasp "a combination of circumstances favorable for the purpose." In other words, opportunity is simply the *potential for success*.

Tapping that potential is your challenge. The question is not whether the strategies and tactics presented in this book provide a *good* opportunity, but whether they provide the *right* opportunity for you. So, using the following criteria, ask yourself these four questions:

- **Purpose**   Do I have the *right* reason(s) for pursuing this opportunity?

- **Timing**   Is this the *right* time for me to do it?

- **Strategy**   Does the *21st Century Financial Practice™* model represent the *right* way for me to capitalize on this opportunity?

- **Humility**   Am I ready to expand my *comfort zone* so I can learn and grow?

At the point where these four elements intersect, you will become aware that the opportunity before you is the "right" one.

Looking For The Right Opportunity

Too many people spend their lives waiting for the right opportunity to come their way. It rarely does, so we suggest that you take a *proactive* approach. It requires initiating a combination of two processes: *anticipation* and *preparation*.

- **Anticipation** –This is the proactive process that enables you to bring the purpose, timing, and strategy elements together. Effective anticipation dramatically increases your capacity to recognize when the intersection of these four elements occurs. Without proper anticipation, you risk spending the rest of your professional life preparing for something that never seems to happen.

- **Preparation** – This is the proactive process of equipping yourself to be ready to act, when the intersection of these four elements occurs. Without adequate preparation, it will not be possible to respond to the opportunities of the 21st century. Timing will become an increasingly critical factor in the years to come.

Anticipation: The Art of Strategic Exploration

As you will soon see, preparation is more of a science while anticipation is an art. Anticipation involves the creative synthesis of information, out of which you will draw some valuable conclusions. It's a way of making sense out of what seems to be an unpredictable future and lifts the fog of uncertainty, producing the "aha!"

Today change comes faster, is more explosive, and is much less predictable. It's not what you do tomorrow, but what you are doing *today* that will determine your ability to survive and be successful *tomorrow*. In that sense, your future is now!

Joel Barker, author of *Paradigms: The Business of Discovering The Future*, describes three keys to the future of any organization that wants to participate fully in the 21st century. *Excellence* and *innovation* are the first two; *anticipation* is the third, which he explains in the following way:

> ***Anticipation*** *provides you with the information that allows you to be in the right place at the right time, with your excellent, innovative product or service. Good anticipation is the result of good **strategic exploration**.*

There are three *critical change factors* at work today that should become the focus of any strategic exploration you do to answer the question, "When should I launch the restructuring of my financial practice?" They are:

Change Factor 1	*What **is** changing*
Change Factor 2	*What **could** change*
Change Factor 3	*What **will likely not** change*

These *critical change factors* are similar to the layers of an onion. We look at the outer layer (What is changing) and:

- If we *have* weathered the storm successfully so far, our resolve to "hang in there" is reinforced.

- If we *have not* weathered the storm very well, regardless of why, we are probably (in varying degrees of desperation) searching for some viable alternative.

Here's the problem! Neither response adequately prepares us for tomorrow's opportunities. Unless we "peel away" the other two layers (critical change factors), it is practically impossible to effectively anticipate and manage the future. The key to good *strategic exploration* is, understanding the interrelationship that exists between the three *critical change factors*.

The interrelationship of these three critical change factors is governed by two important universal principles:

- What *could* change is being shaped by what is changing. In some instances, the *"could"* is actually a predictable extension of the *"is"*. Your decision to change direction should be guided by your constant effort to explore and understand these interrelationships.

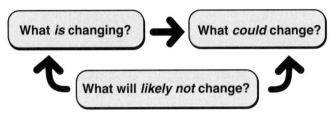

- There are natural laws of human psychology and human interaction that, although influenced by circumstances, remain predictably constant and consistent. Understanding those natural laws will enable you to analyze their interaction with the *"could"* and *"is"* in an effort to predict what will *"likely not change."*

Your effort to strategically explore these three critical change factors and discover how they impact each other, will enable you to see the intersection of purpose, timing, and strategy in your effort to identify tomorrow's opportunities. That effort must become a daily effort. Starting right now, you need to ask "What will tomorrow look like?" You probably do ask that question periodically, but now it needs to be a daily quest, asked in three different ways.

1. **What *is* changing?** This is the easy one, if you stop and take inventory. What changes do you and other Team Members see taking place?

   - With clients

   - Within your company

   - Around the industry

- In the world of business

- On the Internet

- With financial services technology

- Within your own Team

2. **What *could* change?** Expand each of the categories listed above and brainstorm with your Team, considering whether changes you anticipate are predictable, promised, projected, or possible.

3. **What *will likely not* change?** The more effort your Team puts into finding realistic answers to the first two questions, the more clearly you will see the probable answers to this one. The answers to this question are critical to your future success because they define the anchors upon which you can build your business. Those anchors will keep you tied to the important business development, financial advisory, operational efficiency, and client loyalty factors that are most valued by your clients.

Strategic exploration is both energizing and comforting. It gets the creative juices flowing on one hand, while providing the relief of being "in the know" about critical factors that are vital to your success on the other hand. Being able to anticipate the future is great fun!

Preparation: Creating Your Future

As noted earlier, preparation is more of a science than an art. In fact, it can become downright drudgery if it is not synergistically tied to your strategic exploration efforts and driven by your anticipation of the "*is, could, will likely not*" change factors impacting your business. If you've worked on the *21st Century Financial Practice™* strategies and tactics while reading this book, your preparation is well under way.

If you've simply read this book, you've still taken a significant step toward creating your future. The important next step is to begin, one step at a time, to work your way through the strategic thinking and tactical how-to exercises explained in Chapters 3 through 14. We estimate that it will take from 18 months to 2 years to work your way through these exercises and put a *21st Century Financial Practice™* in place.

Opportunity presents itself when anticipation intersects with preparation. Has your humility confirmed a lack of all the answers? Have you determined the right purpose for pursuing this opportunity? Is the timing right? Is our *21st Century Financial Practice™* model the right strategy for you? If your answer is "Yes," we'd love to help you. Let us know how we can.

Matt Oechsli

We also have a comprehensive self-study program with extensive support materials including worksheets and forms for each exercise. For more information, visit our web site at:

http://www.oechsli.com/book

You will find a *Members* Section on the web site for those using the program. It provides additional information plus an opportunity to e-mail questions to us. We invite you to join us. The password for this section is "Affluent21."

References

Barker, J. 1993. *Paradigms: the business of discovering the future.* New York: HarperBusiness.

Brown, M. G. 1996. *Keeping score.* New York: Quality Resources.

Certified Financial Planner Board of Standards. 2001. CFP certificant profile. *www.CFP-board.org.*

Daly, B. 2001. Daytrading for the masses. *Business 2.0*, 29 May, 74-75.

Drucker, P. 1999. *Management challenges for the 21st century.* New York: HarperBusiness.

Financial fixers and fakers. 1998. *Consumers Report*, January, 31-35.

Forbes 400 richest in America. *www.forbes.com. Lists.*

Fox, L. 2001. Heaven can't wait. *Business 2.0*, 20 March, 123-124.

Gardyn, R. 2001. Happiness grows on trees. *American Demographics.* May, 18-21.

Guyton, J. T. 2001. Blazing financial planning's career paths. *Journal of Financial Planning*, April, 150-154.

Hamel, G. 2000. *Leading the revolution.* Boston: Harvard Business School Press.

Harrington, H. J. 1991. *Business process improvement.* New York: McGraw-Hill.

Hurley, M. P., T. G. Fuller, Y. N. Kanner, J. K. Stroh, T. M. Jiede, S. R. Dowl, and P. F. Kobos. 1999. The future of the financial advisory business and the delivery of advice to the semi-affluent investor. *White paper*, Undiscovered Managers, LLC.

Imai, M. 1986. *Kaizen.* New York: McGraw-Hill.

Ivancevich, J. M. and M. T. Matteson. 1996. *Organizational behavior and management.* Chicago: Irwin.

Kaplan, R. S. and D. P. Norton. 1996. *The balanced scorecard.* Boston: Harvard Business School Press.

Kerr, S. 1975. On the folly of rewarding a, while hoping for b. *Academy of Management Journal*, 18: 769-783.

Krantz, L. 2000. *Jobs rated almanac 2001*. New York: St. Martin's Griffin.

Lincoln Financial Group. 2000. The new American millionaires study. www.*LNC.com*.

MacKay, H. 1988. Swim with the sharks without being eaten alive. New York: Random House.

Money Concepts. Why you need an independent financial planner. *www.moneyconcepts.com*.

Observer Column. 2001. Clients more difficult to retain. *Journal of Financial Planning*, April, 26.

——. 2001. Stat bank. *Journal of Financial Planning*, April, 26.

Pickering, C. 2001. Live! From Merrill Lynch? *Business 2.0*, 29 May, 76-77.

Porter, M. 1996. What is strategy. *Harvard Business Review*, November-December.

RR Staff. 2001. Programs aplenty. *Registered Representative*, June, 73-82.

About Matt Oechsli

Matt Oechsli is President of The Oechsli Institute, a firm specializing in servicing the financial services industry. For more than 20 years, he has helped individuals and teams build successful financial advisory practices.

Matt's *How to Build a 21st Century Financial Practice™* has become the premier program for transforming transaction based providers into solutions based Wealth Management Teams that are uniquely equipped to meet the multidimensional needs of the affluent. He has guided more than 600 individuals and teams in their efforts to make this transition, and this book has evolved out of those experiences.

Matt is an accomplished speaker, researcher, coach, and consultant. He has authored two best selling books, and his articles have been published in Registered Representative and numerous other financial services trade publications. Matt also serves on the board of the National Association of Investment Professionals (NAIP).

Matt lives in Greensboro, North Carolina, with his wife and three children.

More Tools To Help You Build Your 21st Century Financial Practice

Matt Oechsli has been providing learning materials and personal coaching for individuals and teams in the financial services industry for more than 20 years – all with an emphasis on enhancing performance. The most current and popular materials can be ordered using the information and Order Form on the following pages.

Additional information regarding speaking, coaching, and other materials can be found at the web site.

www.oechsli.com/book

When visiting the web site, look for these FREE offerings:

- An Assessment Tool to help you evaluate your business.

- An e-mail course: "Your FastTrack To Successfully Attracting and Servicing Affluent Clients".

- A monthly e-mail newsletter: "Total Achievement Update".

Additional Resources and Tools

Creating a Successful 21st Century Financial Practice Kit – $299.00

This self-study program will systematically guide you every step of the way. The KIT includes:
- Game Plan & video / introduction CD
- Four instructional audio cassettes
- Benchmarking & Action Planning booklets
- Fourteen strategic thinking exercises
- Eleven tactical how-to's (including templates for creating your Team's Presentation Folder and Financial Organizer)
- Forty form masters
- Your Financial Advisory Team Guidelines booklet, complete with a Team Agreement template (this is not a legal document)
- Reducing Stress & Visualizing Your Goals – audio cassette No. 5
- Twelve Commandments of a Successful Team – audio cassette No. 6
- Audio cassette review album – 2 cassettes
- And more…

21st Century Financial Practice Assessment Program

Each person is unique. We each approach tasks and goals differently. Our perceptions also differ, and that greatly influences our willingness to make the necessary changes to plan, develop, and implement a successful 21st century financial practice. Behavioral style and attitudinal assessment is available for three important roles…

Sales – includes three reports
- *Selling Behavior Report* – assesses how you are likely to behave in six different selling situations.
- *Selling Attitude Report* – measures attitudes towards key components in the same six selling situations.
- *Sales Success Attitude Profile* – analyzes attitudes toward five areas critical to sales success.

Team Leadership – includes three reports
- *Team Building Profile* – analyzes behavioral style in a team setting.
- *Management Development Report* – measures management aptitudes in six categories.
- *Management Attitude Report* – measures four attitudes considered as critical to management success.

Support Personnel – includes two reports
- *Team Building Profile* – analyzes behavioral style in a team setting.
- *General Employment Report* – assesses key qualities within six categories that shape performance in key support roles.

So that we can customize our assessment program to your specific needs, we ask that you call for more information and prices: 800-883-6582

Winning the Inner Game of Selling – $78.50
Your most important sale is to yourself. Learn how to program your mind for the success you truly want. You will learn how to engage the Achievement Cycle, make your personal 7-7-7 Affirmation Tape, program personal and professional goals into your subconscious mind, consistently step outside your comfort zone, and more.
6 cassette album and 209 page soft cover book

Intangibles Process:
The Psychology of Marketing, Selling & Servicing Intangibles – $44.00
The home study workshop for anyone interested in mastering the psychology of marketing, selling and servicing intangibles. This hardcover workbook offers a complete system for positioning yourself as the "go-to" financial resource in the mind of your prospects. Master the secrets of developing rapport, articulating and demonstrating value, and getting people to want to conduct business with you. Learn how to link every aspect of your marketing, selling, and servicing efforts so you continually feed your pipeline with qualified prospects.
Hardcover Workbook; 249 pages, 19 exercises.

The New Psychology of Selling – $65.00
If you are interested in brushing-up your sales skills, this audio learning system is a must. You will learn the secret of responsive selling by using your prospects strongest motivations. You will also learn how to shift from closing sales to confirming buying decisions. Discover how to turn doubt and tension into sales.
6 audio cassettes

Mind Power for Students – $7.00
A student handbook to help improve studying, build relationships, enhance communication, stimulate motivation, prevent choking on exams, and more. This little gem is a must for any student interested in getting higher grades with less stress. Soft cover, 230 page pocketbook.

Order Form

You may use this form to order by mail or fax.

Description	Qty	Price Ea.	Cost
Creating a Successful 21st Century Financial Practice Kit – *Special Offer* –	_____	$299.00	_____
21st Century Financial Assessment Program	_____	_____	_____
Winning the Inner Game of Selling	_____	$78.50	_____
Intangibles Process: The Psychology of Marketing, Selling & Servicing Intangibles	_____	$44.00	_____
The New Psychology of Selling	_____	$65.00	_____
Mind Power for Students	_____	$7.00	_____
		Sub Total	_____
	NC Resident add 6.5% Sales Tax		_____
		TOTAL	_____

Method of Payment

____ Check – My check for $_____ in U.S. dollars is enclosed.

(payable to The Oechsli Institute)

____ Credit Card

____ AmEx ____ Discover ____ Master Card ____ Visa

Credit Card #: _____ Exp. Date _____

Name on Card: _____

Signature: _____

Required Information

Name_____ Company_____

Address_____

City_____ ST_____ ZIP_____

Work Phone (____)_____ Fax (____)_____

E-Mail_____

To pay by credit card, fax completed form to (336) 273-2342
or call (800) 883-6582.

To pay by check, mail completed form and your check to:

The Oechsli Institute, P.O. Box 29385, Greensboro, NC 27429

Order Form

You may use this form to order by mail or fax.

Description	Qty	Price Ea.	Cost
Creating a Successful 21st Century Financial Practice Kit – *Special Offer* –	_____	$299.00	_____
21st Century Financial Assessment Program	_____	_____	_____
Winning the Inner Game of Selling	_____	$78.50	_____
Intangibles Process: The Psychology of Marketing, Selling & Servicing Intangibles	_____	$44.00	_____
The New Psychology of Selling	_____	$65.00	_____
Mind Power for Students	_____	$7.00	_____
		Sub Total	_____
	NC Resident add 6.5% Sales Tax		_____
		TOTAL	_____

Method of Payment

____ Check – My check for $_____ in U.S. dollars is enclosed.

(payable to The Oechsli Institute)

____ Credit Card

____ AmEx ____ Discover ____ Master Card ____ Visa

Credit Card #: _____ Exp. Date _____

Name on Card: _____

Signature: _____

Required Information

Name_____ Company_____

Address_____

City_____ ST_____ ZIP_____

Work Phone (____)_____ Fax (____)_____

E-Mail_____

To pay by credit card, fax completed form to (336) 273-2342
or call (800) 883-6582.

To pay by check, mail completed form and your check to:

The Oechsli Institute, P.O. Box 29385, Greensboro, NC 27429